PACIFIC AIR COMBAT WW II

VOICES FROM THE PAST

By

HENRY SAKAIDA

ISBN: 0-9625860-7-2

Library of Congress Catalog Card No. 93-084105

Edited by John W. Lambert

Cover Art by John C. Valo

Published by:

Phalanx Publishing Co., Ltd.
1051 Marie Avenue
St. Paul, MN 55118 USA

Printed in the United States of America

PREFACE and ACKNOWLEDGEMENTS

The stories in this book, collected and researched over a twelve year period, involved contributions from many of the actual participants. I did not originally set forth to publish this book. It just evolved as individual mysteries began to be unraveled.

I've always hated mysteries because of my need to know what really happened.

For instance, in 1982 a man in my neighborhood, Mr. Minoru Fujita, asked me a favor. He had been a gunboat skipper at Rabaul during the war. He told me the story of "Keefer", an enemy fighter pilot who had been shot down into the harbor and captured. Fujita gave aid and comfort to this severely wounded flyer; they prayed together, and then he was taken away leaving Fujita with only a name. Did he live or die? What was his real name and where was he from? And more importantly, did his family know what had happened to him? The image of "Keefer" haunted Fujita for over forty-two years. I became obsessed with this unknown pilot because I was so touched by Mr. Fujita's story. It took me seven very frustrating years to find out who "Keefer" was.

Then there was the case of a P-38 pilot who was shot down and captured on Valentine's Day, 1943. I stumbled upon his story quite by accident. While browsing through a Japanese war book given to me by former Zero pilot Kenji Yanagiya (the sole surviving escort on the Yamamoto Mission) I saw a reference to a shot down P-38 pilot, name unknown. It mentioned that he was a twenty-two year old second lieutenant and a graduate of Michigan University. Those were the only clues I needed to prompt my research. I identified the pilot as twenty-two year old Second Lieutenant Wellman H. Huey of Detroit, Michigan. He had attended the University of Michigan. I had to search for Wellman's next of kin so that I could tell them this story. I'm sure you would have done the same. Wellman's story can now be told, thanks to former Zero pilot Ryoji Ohara of Yokosuka, Japan. They had met face-to-face.

Other mysteries were solved through the hard work of others. Take the case of the Yamamoto Mission. For more than forty years the public was led to believe that Captain Thomas Lanphier Jr. was the pilot who had shot down Admiral Isoroku Yamamoto. This one event helped change the course of the Pacific War.

"So who cares whether Captain Lanphier or Lieutenant Rex Barber shot down Yamamoto?" you may ask.

History cares. Our history should record the truth, giving credit where credit is due. A great historical injustice was perpetrated on Rex Barber, the man who actually shot down Admiral Yamamoto. The truth is often there for anyone willing to seek it, and it is never too late to set the record straight.

Tales of humanity by enemy combatants, both in the air and on the ground, have always fascinated me. Even during wars, soldiers have risen above hate to show this enviable human trait. I've tried to record some of the more interesting stories - the ones you may never read about in history books.

The men in these stories who did their duty and participated in creating history are, for the most part, "regular Joes". They could be your neighbor . Most of them are in their seventies now. I tried to include photographs of them as they appeared during the war and now. It happens to satisfy my own curiosity: "What do they look like and what are they doing today?"

I have a most unusual hobby of reuniting former enemy pilots from World War II. I had a first taste of this when I helped reunite former Luftwaffe General Adolf Galland with the American P-47 pilot who disabled his Me-262 jet high over the Danube in April 1945. Galland was a great fighter-leader, highly decorated, and an ace with 104 aerial victories to his credit. Jim Finnegan, a jovial Irishman and private investigator, met his old opponent at San Francisco International Airport in 1980. Galland still carries metal splinters in his knee from their first meeting, but there were no hard feelings.

On Memorial Day in 1982 I engineered a reunion between Zero pilot Saburo Sakai and several U.S. Navy dive bomber crewmen who severely wounded him over Guadalcanal in 1942; Sakai lost his right eye and struggled for nearly five hours to reach home. Sakai met Harold L. Jones - one of eight SBD tail gunners shooting at him. Sakai put 232 holes in Jones' SBD and nearly killed him, but belly armor saved his life.

Lew Jones and his wife run a popular bed and breakfast inn located in the picturesque ghost town of Unionville, Nevada. Also at this reunion was Harold P. Newell, a CPA from Northern California and the Hellcat pilot who shot down Sakai's comrade and protege - the great veteran "ace" Hiroyoshi Nishizawa, once Japan's top ace.

Robert A. Weatherup from San Jose, California was also there. Sakai actually saw Weatherup shoot down another of his comrades - Shoichi Sugita - whose story appears in this book.

In all of these reunions and correspondences between former enemies I was struck by the fact that there was absolutely no animosity. With the passing of time did these old warriors mellow? Probably, but the real answer is that they were simply professionals doing their jobs without personal hatred for their foe.

Perhaps aviators are a different breed of soldier. The love of flying and adventure are their common bonds. And what do they talk about when they meet? Shop talk - about the hardships at the front, the lousy chow, the time they almost "bought it" , their aircraft, old comrades, and how lucky they were to survive. They compliment each other on their flying ability and laugh and joke like old squadronmates. I get a real kick out of that.

By dissecting battles, identifying units and individual participants and showing the aftermath I hope to bring the horrors of war to a personal level. Captain Robert W. Wilson of VMF-222 shot down a Zero over Tobera Airfield (Rabaul) on March 12, 1944. By itself this fact does not have much impact on the reader. However, I have identified the Zero pilot killed in action that day as Petty Officer Munetoshi Harada.

Colonel Wilson writes, "At the time, those actions seemed very impersonal - it was man (me) against a machine (him). But when you put the name of the Japanese as Harada, it makes it so human. Having lived in Japan and met so many fine young men there, it all seems so pointless." That's precisely what I'm trying to convey.

I wish I could take credit for writing this book, but the real credit goes to the participants for whom it is dedicated.

* * *   * * *   * * *

I am very indebted to a great number of people and organizations for their kind contributions. I owe my greatest appreciation to Mr. Jiro Yoshida of Tokyo, Japan. He acted as liaison between myself and the surviving Japanese Zero pilots. As a former Zero pilot himself he has helped promote goodwill and friendship between Japan and the U.S. through his foreign exchange student program called J.A.C.E. (Japan - American Cultural Exchange).

Jack Lambert, my publisher, provided great enthusiasm and support. He, together with Jim VanNada and the Seventh Fighter Command Association, were instrumental in arranging a most unusual reunion in Hawaii between two former enemy pilots, whose story appears in this book.

Dr. Yasuho Izawa of Tokyo has guided my research efforts through the years. His loan of precious photographs and intimate knowledge of the history of Japanese Navy and Army Air Forces were invaluable.

Shori Tanaka, a master model builder and photographer, worked tirelessly to provide me with life-like aircraft depictions. His work is so flawless, his depictions have often been mistaken for original combat photographs.

Alexander "Lex" McAulay of Australia was very generous of his time and expertise. He helped me solve the "Keefer" mystery which had stymied me for over seven years. He saved my sanity which helped tremendously in completing this book.

Robert K. Piper is another fine Aussie who did all he could to help, especially in matters relating to the Australian efforts in the Rabaul area. Thank you, mate.

Barrett Tillman, a respected aviation writer and mentor, co-authored the story of LBJ's Silver Star. He helped publish my first book, **Winged Samurai**, in 1985. His contribution and guidance were of great help.

Translations of Japanese documents, letters, and articles posed the biggest problem for me. Fortunately, my father, Tadashi Sakaida, lent me a hand and encouraged me to study and learn Japanese (to get me off his back). Minoru Fujita, my neighbor, was very gracious in providing me with precise translations. His service in the Japanese Imperial Navy and his knowledge of proper military terminology were of great help. He also helped me draft letters to veterans in Japan.

I am grateful to the following individuals for their unselfish help and generosity:
Robert M. Applegate, Major General Alan J. Armstrong, USMC (Ret.), Mrs. Esther Ashley, Colonel Rex Barber, the late Captain Marshall U. Beebe, Steven Blake, Edward Bollen, the late Gregory "Pappy" Boyington, Mary R. Broadhurst, Gregg Butsumyo, Vice Admiral Malcolm W. Cagle, Doug Canning, the late General Charles Chandler, Trevor Coker, Howard R. Commons, Bryan B. Cox, Jim Crossley, Mrs. Eleanor Dunn, John Ebel, Tom Foote, Walt Gaylor, Wiley A. Green, Hayden A. Gregory, Raymond F. "Hap" Halloran, Miki Hayasaki and family, Aloysius X. Hiltgen, the late Major Yohei Hinoki, Jose L. Holguin, Bruce D. Hoy, Tomoyoshi Hori, Don H. Huey and family, Donald J. Humphrey, the late Edward Hymoff, Banshichi Iino, Yoshiro Ikari, Tomoichi Kasai, Masao Kikuchi (Editor, Maru Magazine), Sadamu Komachi, Captain William F. Krantz, USN (Ret.), Walter A. Krell, Yasuo Kumoi, the late Forrest McCormick, Henry Meigs II, Haruko Shirakata Mihara, Edward H. Mikes Jr., Robert Millington, Masahiro Mitsuda, Yasumasa Miyasaka, Gene Monihan, Yutaka Morioka, Robert F. Mulhollem, Kiyoko Muto, Mike O'Connor, Ryoji Ohara, Frank Olynyk, Denny D. Pidhayny, Don "Buttercup" Pryor, Saburo Sakai, Ronald R. Sathre, William J. Satzer, Robert S. Scamara, John C. Sellman, the late J. Clifford Shaw and his wife Marian, Yoshio Shiga and the 343rd Kokutai Association, the Shiro Shimizu family, Mayumi Shirakata, Art T. Siordia, Michiko and Terrance Smart, R.T. Smith, F.R. Stevens, Jr., Captain Sir Robert A.G. Strickland, Dr. Hiroya Sugano, Takeo Tanimizu, Lloyd R. Tatum, Tatsuya Mike Terasaki, Colonel Raymond F. Toliver, Staff Sgt. Albert Tyree, Robert A. Weatherup, Malcolm C. Watters, Laverle H. Westerman, John T. Wible, Colonel Robert M. Wilson, USMC (Ret.), Kenji Yanagiya, and Masahiro Yoshimatsu.

The following organizations also deserve to be recognized: Admiral Nimitz Museum, American Legion, Australian Archives, Australian War Memorial, Marine Corps Aviation Association, National Archives, Naval

Aviation Museum Foundation, The Naval Historical Center, New Zealand Defense Force, P-38 National Association, RAAF Historical Section, Smithsonian Institution, The Tailhook Association, U.S. Marine Corps, U.S. Naval Institute, U.S.A.F. Historical Research Center, Veterans of Foreign Wars and the Zero Fighter Pilots Association.

If I have missed anyone, please accept my apologies. Thank you all for helping me save some interesting bits of history.

Temple City, California
April 1, 1993

HENRY SAKAIDA

TABLE OF CONTENTS

TOUGHEST FIGHTER PILOT IN THE IMPERIAL NAVY

"Kaneyoshi Muto was the toughest fighter pilot in the Imperial Navy," exclaimed legendary Zero ace Saburo Sakai. "He had peerless skills."

Others likened him to a famous medieval swordsman who could kill with one stroke of the sword. He disappeared on a combat mission two weeks before the end of the war. Today's Japanese care very little for their war heroes, but in order to appreciate ours, we must look at warriors of the other side. Our fighter pilots fought a very tough war, and Kaneyoshi Muto was one of the reasons.

He was born June 18, 1916 in Aichi Prefecture, Honshu, Japan. His widow Kiyoko reflects on his childhood.

"His parents were farmers and he was the third son in a family of five boys and two elder sisters. He didn't fight with his brothers and as a grammar school student he was very studious. When he was in the fifth grade his parents sent him to his uncle to be raised for the priesthood. But he tired of the rigorous training and changed his mind. He returned home in about a year and attended school in Tsushima.

"My husband was very short. When he was riding his bicycle he had a very difficult time because his legs were short and he barely reached the pedals. He would ride his bicycle about eight kilometers to school every day on a gravel road. When he was in the eighth grade he quit school but really had no idea what he wanted to do with his life. He thought about becoming a teacher and worked briefly in a bakery but didn't like it and quit. He then enlisted in the Navy."

On June 1, 1935 nineteen year old Kaneyoshi joined the Navy at Kure Naval Station. After basic training he served briefly aboard the destroyer **Uranami**. He realized that becoming an aviator would advance his career, so he applied to become a flight trainee. He was accepted and commenced training at Kasumigaura Air Base on January 21, 1936. He graduated on July 28, 1936 and was posted to Omura Air Base as an instructor for incoming flight trainees.

The China War began on July 7, 1937 when Japanese troops clashed with the Chinese on the Marco Polo Bridge near Beijing. The Japanese quickly occupied Beijing on July 28th and laid siege to Shanghai the following month. Muto was transferred to the 12th Kokutai (air group) based in China and scored his first aerial victory on December 4, 1937 when he shot down a Russian built I-16 fighter over Nanking. In the face of the Japanese blitzkrieg Generalissimo Chiang Kai-shek, leader of the Chinese Nationalists, gave orders to evacuate Nanking. The great city fell five days later and over 200,000 defenders were killed. Chiang moved his headquarters to Hankow along with remnants of his air force. The 12th Kokutai was China's main fighter opposition. Muto engaged in some hard fighting in and around Hankow. As a result he received an official commendation on April 30, 1938. He left the battle front with at least five aerial victories and returned to Japan in December to become an instructor.

When the Pacific War began on December 8, 1941 Muto was flying with the 3rd Kokutai. He flew as

Wedding photo of Muto and his new bride in 1942.

wingman to Lieutenant Tomotsu Yokoyama during the raid on Iba and Clark Fields in the Philippines. Muto also participated in the attacks over Manila and advanced with his unit to the Dutch East Indies. With the end of the Malayan Campaign, Muto returned again to Japan in April 1942.

The euphoria of victory filled the air. Japan was in its heyday in the Spring of 1942, her mighty military machine seemingly invincible. The Zero fighter was the undisputed master of the sky. Petty Officer First Class Muto had now found his niche in life. A promotion in May 1942 was followed by another commendation for distinguished service in the Philippines Campaign. He was given a well deserved leave and his widow, Kiyoko, recalls their first meeting:

"We were introduced through a third party. I remember it was some time in May 1942, around six in the morning. He had come home from the South Pacific. One day while on furlough he showed up at our house with another gentleman. My mother was surprised and invited them in and served refreshments. They didn't stay very long, but we were formally introduced then. On October 12, 1942 we were married. He was not present at our wedding because he was off fighting again. The two families met and the marriage ceremony was performed. Later we pasted our individual photographs together to make a wedding portrait."

Japan's "invincible" Navy suffered a devastating defeat at the Battle of Midway on June 4-5, 1942 from which she never fully recovered. Four carriers and over 250 aircraft and hundreds of prewar trained pilots were lost. Japan's war machine switched from offensive to defensive and the need to replace pilot losses became critical. Entrance requirements were lowered and many trainees were inducted from the ordinary ranks. Pilot quality plummeted.

Muto transferred to the 252 Kokutai and advanced to the great bastion at Rabaul on New Britain Island. From his arrival aboard the carrier **Taiyo** on November 9, 1942 until March 1943 he engaged in fierce combats in Eastern New Guinea and the Solomons. On April 6th he received a military decoration for distinguished service.

It was inevitable that Muto would become an instructor again. Japan had not recovered from the calamity at Midway and the Solomons Campaign further decimated the thinning ranks of veteran pilots. The few who survived formed the cadre of the instructor corps. Muto was transferred to the Yokosuka Kokutai in September 1943.

Yokosuka Kokutai was Japan's oldest naval air group and a coveted assignment. It served as the guardian of the Imperial Capital. Muto was promoted to warrant officer on November 1st. Back on the mainland again, his new duty station reunited him with his wife.

Kiyoko Muto recalls: "He didn't talk much about the war or about his plans after the war, as it dragged on and on, and things became very unfavorable for Japan. But my husband had a cheerful disposition and he was very understanding. He liked to read and even at war or at home he read many books and understood many things...In December 1943, we started a new life."

The assignment to Yokosuka Kokutai reunited Muto with an old China hand - Saburo Sakai. Badly wounded over Guadalcanal in August 1942, Sakai was sent back to Japan for further hospitalization. Despite the loss of his right eye Sakai was still good enough to be an instructor. It was very frustrating for such veterans to serve in the instructor's role. Forced into a mass production mode, young pilots were thrown into combat after basic training and very few survived. Both men hated being part of it.

By June 1944 the Americans were preparing to take the Marianas seizing the three main islands of Saipan, Guam and Tinian. The Japanese planned a counter offensive called Operation "A-Go" and the Yokosuka Kokutai was rushed to the harsh volcanic island of Iwo Jima to implement the strategy. Muto and Sakai were ecstatic to get out of training and into combat.

On June 24, 1944 Iwo Jima was raided by U.S. Navy carrier borne Hellcats. Muto and Sakai fought furiously, each claiming several victories, but their unit's losses were staggering. The severe beating forced the high command to order a desperate, one way suicide mission (Kamikaze) for the remaining pilots. Muto and Sakai were aghast to be sacrificed in such a futile attempt. As enlisted men they had no choice but to follow orders.

Muto relaxes by his Zero in this pre-1945 photo.

On July 5th they departed on the first suicide mission against the U.S. fleet but were bounced by Hellcats before they could locate any targets. They brought back their wingmen against overwhelming odds. In just three battles, Yokosuka Kokutai lost over twenty-two veteran pilots and almost all of their aircraft. Although the unit claimed an incredible fifty-two victories there was no cause for celebration. The remaining pilots were evacuated by transport planes back to the mainland.

Muto came back and flew air defense around the Tokyo region. However, his unit did not witness combat again until the first Marianas based B-29s raided Tokyo on November 24, 1944. This attack was followed by four more raids before the end of the year.

For the first time since the Doolittle Raiders bombed Tokyo in 1942, Americans were returning to the Imperial Capitol in force. The token raid by Doolittle's B-25s had just been an audacious slap in the face. The upcoming carrier raid on Tokyo was to be a devastating uppercut. The Fast Carrier Force (Task Force 58) under the command of naval aviation expert, Vice Admiral Marc Mitscher, maneuvered into position for a morning assault on Tokyo slated for February 16, 1945. Looking forward to action that day was thirty year old Lieutenant Hayden Alvin Gregory of VF-82 aboard carrier **Bennington**.

At 1106 sixteen F6F-5s roared off from the Bennington. It was the second strike of the day, the dawn mission being the first flight ever made by carrier air groups over the Japanese homeland. VF-82 was still charged up and spoiling for a fight.

Enroute to the target, Ensign P.L. Stradling from Gregory's division was forced to abort due to engine malfunction. The division leader, Lieutenant James F. Carroll, ordered Ensign Carl C. Dace to escort Stradling back. Stradling was shot down by trigger happy gunners aboard the escort was destroyed when he failed to make a circular identification turn. The fourteen remaining Hellcats continued on course with other units to the Tokyo Bay area, arriving over Atsugi Naval Airfield.

"Buck" Gregory in his Hellcat on the Bennington.

Lieutenant Commander Edward W. Hessel, VF-82 CO, led his four plane division down through the overcast and attacked the enemy airfield with good results. Lieutenants Gregory and Carroll, both of whom lost their wingmen enroute, had paired up and were diving when their troubles began. A Japanese fighter was making a run on Gregory's wingman.

Gregory recalls the events of that combat: "During our melee a stray plane from our squadron who had become separated from his flight joined our four. I never knew who it was. I was on the tail of what I thought was the last enemy plane. Just as I flamed it, I was hit by 20mm from a plane on my tail. I lost several feet of one wing and an opposite elevator. At this time another stray from our squadron joined the battle and shot down the plane which

Lieutenant James F. Carroll.

Ensign Earl A. McAllister, Jr.

had hit me. He escorted me back to the carrier. I managed to land aboard with the damaged plane. But it was damaged too severely and was pushed over the side. The pilot who had saved me was Ensign Earl McAllister Jr. (He became my wingman when the flights were reassigned, and I lost him on a later mission to ground fire while we were strafing airfields in the northern Japanese islands.) On this flight my gun camera credited me with one Frank and one Tojo destroyed with three probables."

Head-on or over the shoulder, this is a frontal view of the Kawanishi NIK2-J, George. (Depicted by Shori Tanaka)

The Japanese fighters belonged to the Yokosuka Kokutai. A mixed group of Zeros, Shiden-Kai (George) and Raiden (Jack) fighters, under the command of Lieutenant Yuzo Tsukamoto (deceased 1991), were eager to redeem themselves for their humiliating defeat over Iwo Jima. They hurled themselves at the American foes, with Muto piloting a George from the evaluation department of his air group.

The George - Kawanishi N1K2-J Shiden-Kai - was the newest navy fighter to enter combat. It was better than or equal to the Grumman Hellcat in performance. Armed with four 20 mm cannons, it had armor protection, and an automatic combat flap system that enabled it to turn on a dime.

In the engagement of 16 February 1945 seven VF-82 pilots had encountered ten Japanese fighters in a wild dogfight. The VF-82 mission report stated, "Each of our pilots who saw the fight joined in, weaving and 'fighting in the same air'. This fight took place just below the overcast and it is believed that this forced the Jap into using the same tactics of 'fighting in the same air' whether they planned such tactics or not. Atsugi is an army (sic) fighter training field and it is entirely possible that Jap pilots were combat experienced instructors from this field. At any rate, these Jap pilots were good marksmen and seemed to use good tactics."

The fighting skill of the Japanese pilots came as a rude shock to the Americans. Ensign Charles A. McCrea, Jr. was jumped by a very aggressive Japanese who clung to him like glue and hammered on him. "I was jumped by a 'Jack' and could not outmaneuver him. At 7,000 feet, I did a roll and headed seaward with the Jack on my tail. He chased me for fifteen miles but could not overtake me," reported McCrea in his report. He landed safely aboard the carrier with .50 caliber holes in his right wing but didn't return empty handed. He claimed two Zeros.

The combat between VF-82 and the Yokosuka Kokutai evolved into the famous and often repeated "twelve against one" episode. According to the popular Japanese story, Muto (by this time promoted to Ensign) singlehandedly challenged twelve Hellcats over Atsugi and shot down four of them before the Americans fled the area. Government radio broadcasts gave credence to this story in an attempt to create an instant hero and boost public morale.

Kiyoko Muto was very surprised to hear her husband's incredible deed. She recalls, "When I heard the news on the radio, I was so proud of him."

Muto made headlines that day and his name became a household word. The press call him "Miyamoto Musashi of the Air" in reference to Japan's greatest swordsman of the medieval era. In fact, four VF-82 Hellcats were lost in combat, but it will never be known how many fell to Muto.

The loss of four pilots in this encounter was a devastating blow to the Squadron. Lieutenant James F. Carroll scored a victory before he was hit and parachuted but he was never seen again. Lieutenant Benjamin A. Inghram was hit in the oil system and was forced to ditch his plane in Tokyo Bay. He succeeded in getting into his rubber raft and was last seen cheerfully waving to his comrades overhead. Lieutenants Robert H. Jennings Jr. and Elbert S. Heim circled Inghram for over two hours before dwindling fuel forced them to leave. Lieutenant Jennings radioed for a submarine, but was turned down. Inghram had come down in a restricted area that was off limits to submarines. A rescue attempt would have been too risky. Inghram was never recovered.

Lieutenant David O. Puckett, Jr. and Ensign James A. McCann were last seen in aerial combat over Atsugi.

Ensign Charles A. McCrea, Jr.

Ensign James A. McCann

They were listed as missing in action, but both turned up in a POW camp. Puckett now resides in Mississippi but McCann disappeared into civilian life. "Buck" Gregory scored his fifth and last victory on April 6, 1945 and joined the fraternity of aces. He served in the postwar navy, retired, and now makes his home in New Mexico.

When the second big carrier raid against Tokyo was launched the following day, February 17, the Yokosuka Kokutai and Kaneyoshi Muto were once again in heated combat. The unit claimed nineteen enemy aircraft destroyed with another six probables. Due to the destruction of records their losses for the two days are unknown.

In June, 1945 Captain Minoru Genda commanding officer of the 343 Kokutai called for Muto to join his unit down on Shikoku. He was to replace another great veteran, Ensign Shoichi Sugita who had been killed on April 15, 1945.

The war was drawing to a close. The majority of veteran pilots were dead, and those who had survived were being sacrificed in futile suicide attacks in the Philippines and Okinawa. Complaints were now being heard from American Navy pilots about the scarcity of action. In the month between June 9 and July 9 they made no aerial victory claims. It was widely believed that the quality of Japanese fighter pilots had deteriorated to the point where they offered no serious opposition.

Unknown to the Americans, there was plenty of sting left in certain elite units. On July 24, 1945 at 0800 hours, eight F6F-5s and four F4U Corsairs took off from the **Yorktown** for the great Kure Naval Base. This attack was part of a massive aerial strike to cut the jugular of the badly hemorrhaging Japanese Navy. Several hundred aircraft from eight carriers flew over the south coast of

Lieutenant Benjamin A. Inghram

Shikoku Island at 12,000 feet before reaching the target area. Flying on this mission was Lieutenant Malcolm W. Cagle of VF-88.

The **Yorktown** group consisting of Hellcats and Corsairs with #500 GP bombs, and TBM Avengers rained their deadly ordnance down on the Japanese fleet at anchor. A heavy barrage of anti-aircraft fire dotted the sky with colorful (and deadly) puffs of red, brown, yellow, and black smoke.

Lieutenant (jg) Thompson of VF-88 made a 60 degree dive at 330 knots and released his bomb at 4,000 feet on the cruiser **Oyodo**. He scored a hit about forty feet in from the bow. Ensign Ted Hansen, the fourth man down, laid his bomb squarely on the rear of the ship. Lieutenant Cagle and his wingman, Lieutenant (jg) Ken Neyer followed the Avengers of VT-88 down on the cruiser **Tone**. The torpedo planes made their hits and the two Hellcats pushing over from 12,000 feet, released their

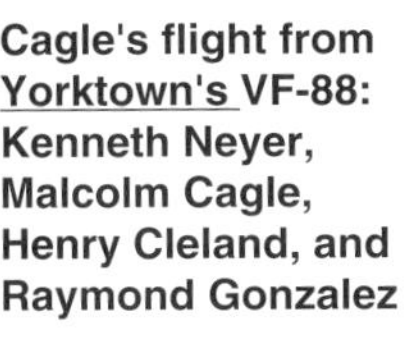

Cagle's flight from Yorktown's VF-88: Kenneth Neyer, Malcolm Cagle, Henry Cleland, and Raymond Gonzalez

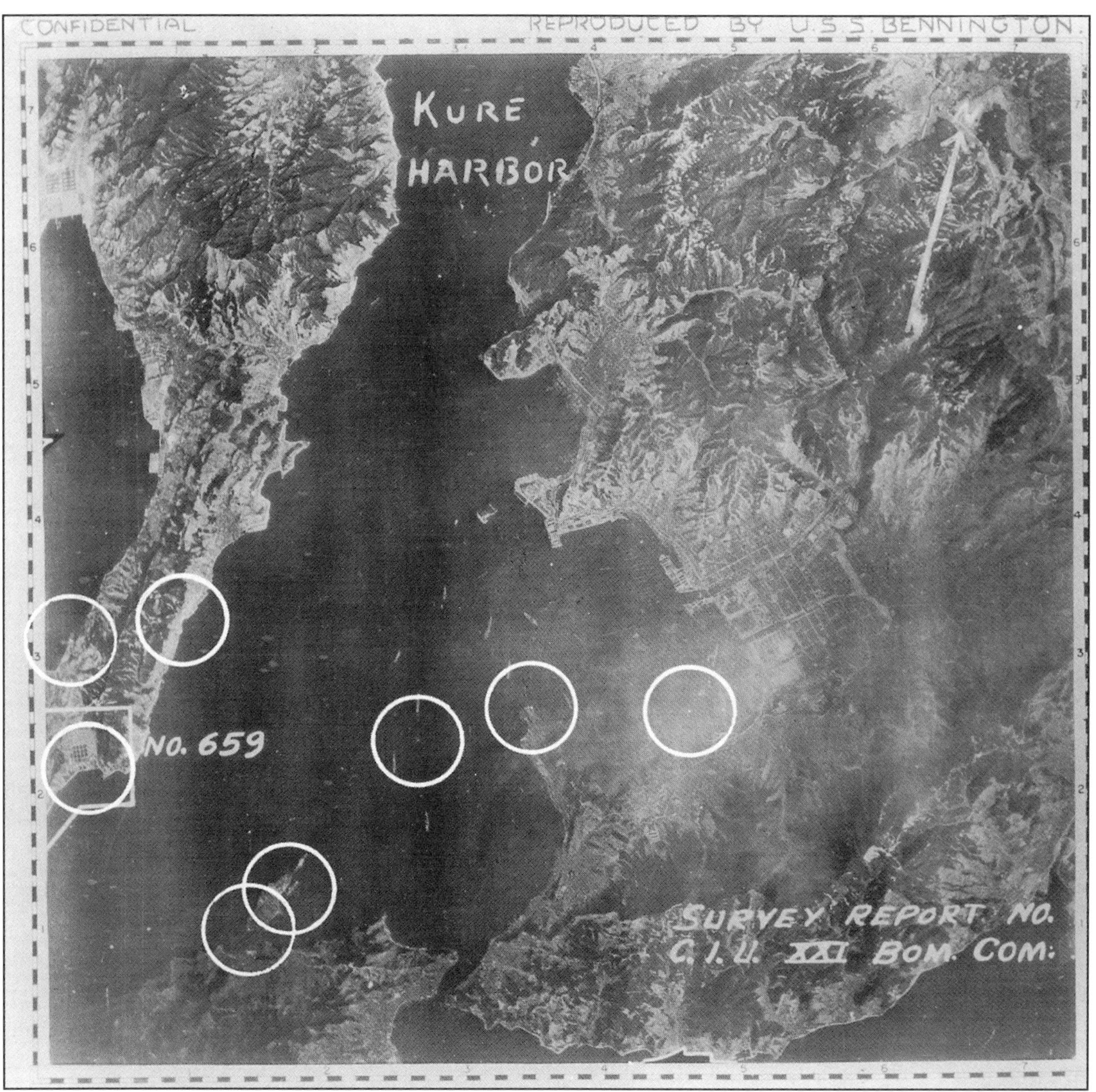

Kure just prior to the big strike of July 24, 1945. Primary targets have been circled.

bombs at 3,500 feet to add some finishing touches. Cagle scored a direct hit on the **Tone** and the Air Group began retirement to a rendezvous point through the Bungo Strait.

The massive American raid over Kure was being monitored at Genda's headquarters where three squadrons from the 343rd Kokutai totaling twenty-one Shiden-Kai Georges were scrambled. Captain Genda directed them to strike at the enemy as they retreated seaward to their carriers. He believed that having expended their ordnance and considerable fuel the American aircraft were now most vulnerable to his fighters.

Ensign Kaneyoshi Muto flew with the 301 Squadron under the leadership of Lieutenant Naoshi Kanno, another veteran ace. This was Muto's first mission with the new unit and it would be his last, but details would not be known until 1981.

The 301st made contact with the Americans around 1005 near Mizunoko Island lighthouse when they caught two Corsairs of VBF-1 lagging behind a formation of Avengers heading home. Lieutenant Shoji Matsumura led his flight toward the TBMs up ahead while Muto and his men went after the more challenging F4Us.

Lieutenant (jg) Robert M. Applegate, one of the two Corsair pilots, recalls what happened:

"We were all throttled back and when I saw these four planes come across us I was about a mile behind my squadron with my wingman, Ensign Robert J. Speckman. They just bracketed us and made a beautiful run. I saw Speckman going down in a ball of fire - that guy took him out on the first run."

Applegate was now in the worst possible situation. He was alone and under attack. It was then that Lieutenant Cagle and his wingman arrived on the scene. Cagle had spotted aircraft milling around in the distance but did not recognize that a dogfight was in progress until he saw a plane explode, burn, and go down.

Cagle recalls, "At that last stage of the war we had no idea that the Japanese had much left to fight with. It was our impression that their Kamikaze attacks, using largely untested and poorly trained pilots, was about all they could put in the air. And our information about the new Japanese fighters was very scant."

Vastly outnumbered, Cagle made the only decision possible - he and Neyer charged into the fray.

As soon as the two Hellcats were spotted, the Georges immediately commenced simultaneous high stern runs, coordinating to catch both in a cross pattern. Cagle and Neyer began a Thach weave for mutual protection but the Japanese were all over them. Ken Neyer was hit and disappeared.

Applegate made a 180 degree turn and opened up with a sixty degree deflection shot into the second plane of the enemy section. He saw his tracers hitting the engine and in the fuselage around the cockpit. The George started smoking, rolled over on its back, and dived straight down. He started to follow, but his own plane started to spin. He recovered, only to find another George jockeying right behind him. Instinctively, Applegate wrapped his Corsair into a very tight turn. The George pilot clung to his tail, not more than a few yards behind, trying desperately to lead his fire into the American. Applegate looked back and could see the enemy pilot hunched behind the controls concentrating intently on his demise. He believed that he had just seconds to live when he saw a Hellcat maneuvering behind his opponent and pieces flying off the George. His guardian angel was Malcolm Cagle who was placing hits between the engine and cockpit. Cagle put several long bursts into the tail with a zero to fifteen degrees deflection shot. There was an explosion and a burst of flame from the George's engine. Applegate recalls, "The entire tail section just vanished and he went in."

The grateful Corsair pilot signaled to the Hellcat pilot and the pair started a Thach weave out of the channel. There was one George left and it made a high side run on Applegate from four o'clock and instead of pulling back up, continued on across the Corsair and Hellcat and turned back in a beam run from ten o'clock. The weave placed Applegate in a position to make a head-on pass at the enemy aircraft.

"He came in on a head-on run and I began shooting," said Applegate. "I had earlier shot up a small boat and expended a lot of ammo, which was a bad mistake on my part. I ran out of ammo as we closed. I felt he was trying to ram me."

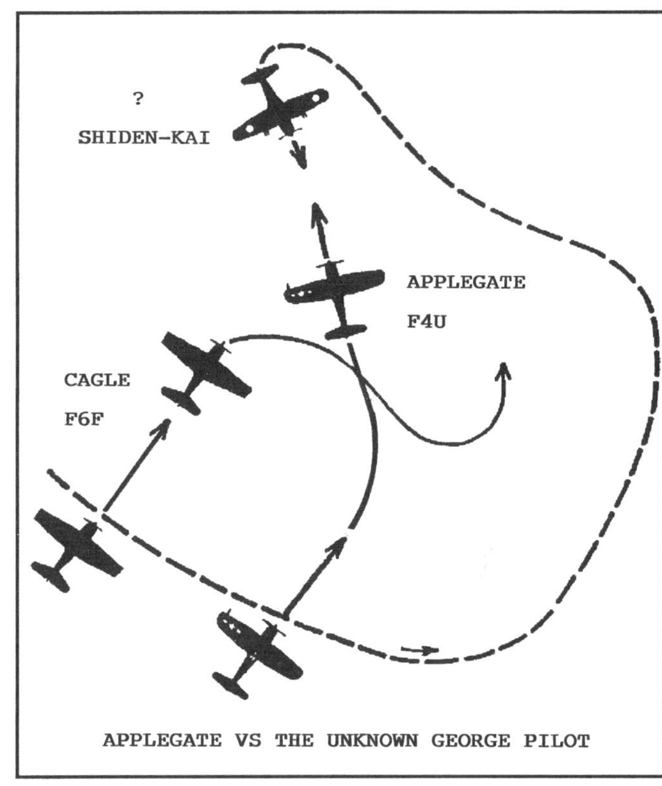

APPLEGATE VS THE UNKNOWN GEORGE PILOT

A Bennington Corsair of Air Group One preparing to launch for a strike against the Japanese mainland.

Tracers from the Corsair were seen hitting the nose of the George and Applegate felt his own engine take five or six hits. He pushed his plane down and the George cleared his canopy by less than ten feet. With the enemy pilot slumped forward, Applegate got a fleeting glimpse of the George rolling over and disappearing. Now the two Americans had lost track of each other in the final frenzied encounter.

The Corsair was spurting black smoke from its engine. Applegate decided to dump his crate. Bailing out, he struck himself on the tail plane but luckily suffered no broken bones.

He recalls, "I thought I had opened the chute too soon because I ripped out two panels. Then I hit the water. I might have been about 500 feet when I went over the side. The groundcrew had packed my gear wrong because when I tried to get the rubber raft out I had much difficulty. Finally I got my knife and cut it out. In the process I stabbed myself in the left arm, right through to the bone."

Applegate managed to climb into his life raft and had high hopes of being rescued. "I figured I'd be seen since we were in the first strike of the day and there were to be others. Then the next day, another strike. I put the dye marker in the water and used my signal mirror, but nothing. Toward night I heard a plane so I fired my flare gun. Shore gunners opened up on me. The next morning I found a piece of stick and made it into a sail. I set my anchor and waited. No one seemed to have spotted me. Two mines floated by.

"Then I saw two Hellcats going along the shore. They were looking for one of their own pilots but found me instead. They never did find their buddy, but they contacted a submarine which finally surfaced near me. One of the crewmen threw me a line and said to hang on for all it's worth. He said, 'Hang on tight. The last pilot who let go got chopped up in the propeller.' The sub was going full speed out of the mine field and I felt like I was water skiing."

"They told me to go down below. I took two steps and fell on my face. I was paralyzed below the waist and my legs gave out. They grabbed me and literally dropped me into the hatch."

Robert Applegate spent about a month on board the USS **Dragonet** (SS-293) before he was returned to his squadron. Cagle returned safely to the Yorktown. Shortly after the war, the two met again and Applegate thanked his benefactor for saving his life.

Nobuya Yoneda (left) and Susumu Imai were both lost on July 24th defending Kure.

Rodney Tabler (left) and Robert Speckman fell victims to Muto's flight.

When the Japanese pilots returned to base, three pilots from the 301 Squadron were missing: Ensign Kaneyoshi Muto, Chief Petty Officer Nobuya Yoneda, and Petty Officer Second Class Susumu Imai. Total 343rd Kokutai losses for the day were six planes and pilots while the unit claimed sixteen F4Us, F6Fs, and SB2Cs.

Ensign Arlen C. Davis (left) and Robert M. Applegate slice a "Welcome Back" cake aboard <u>Bennington</u>.

American losses (combat and operational) amounted to six F4Us, three F6Fs, six TBMs, and 13 SB2Cs, a total of twenty-eight aircraft. U.S. Navy pilots claimed nine kills, two probables, and two damaged in this action. VBF-1 lost three aircraft and two pilots (Lieutenant Rodney C. Tabler and Ensign Robert J. Speckman).

In 1981, Kiyoko Muto was informed regarding some of the details of her husband's last combat. In her letter she writes, "I never knew what had happened to my husband. He went out and never came back." After more than thirty-six years she finally knew and was very grateful.

Could the lone George pilot who made the head-on run against Applegate have been Muto? According to Applegate, this pilot was either very brave or very foolish. Saburo Sakai, who knew Muto's style, remarked, "That pilot could not have been Muto. He would never have made such a foolish head-on attack."

On November 15, 1978 a diver discovered a George lying 130 feet down in Hido Bay. Subsequent research revealed that it had belonged to the 301 Squadron and that it was ditched by its pilot on July 24, 1945. The aircraft was salvaged on July 14, 1979. An eyewitness was located who had rowed a boat out to rescue the pilot. He stated that the pilot could be seen in the cockpit as the plane slid under. The George was found with the canopy closed. When it was examined no remains of the pilot were found.

It is theorized that the pilot managed to survive for a short time utilizing his oxygen mask or an air pocket in the cockpit. When he tried to exit the aircraft in his wounded condition he drowned and his body was swept away. Strong tidal action closed the canopy.

Kaneyoshi Muto (he preferred the nickname "Kinsuke") was officially declared killed in action July 24, 1945. He received a posthumous promotion to the rank of lieutenant junior grade. There are no records to determine the number of enemy aircraft he destroyed in combat. Saburo Sakai comments, "He didn't have a high score in comparison to other aces I knew. However, I believe he scored over thirty victories."

Muto had a very long and distinguished career and missed surviving the war by a couple of weeks. At the time of his death his only child, a daughter named Yoshiko, was not quite five months old. Mrs. Muto now resides in Aichi Prefecture with her daughter and three grandchildren.

Malcolm Cagle retired from the navy as a vice admiral and lives in Virginia. He raises a purebred herd of 130 cows, calves and bulls on 417 acres in the beautiful foothills of the Blue Ridge. At age seventy-four he still has the stamina to chase down a stray heifer.

Robert Applegate returned to Japan in 1987 with his wife. He writes, "One of the highlights for me was leaving Kobe by ship and sailing down the Inland Sea very near the place where I was shot down. The lighthouse is still there (probably not the same one) but nothing else looked even vaguely familiar. The only reason I could locate anything was the navigator let me look at the charts, but it was a thrill anyway. Japan is as beautiful as I remember and the people are still pleasant and polite." Bob Applegate retired as a city manager and now resides in El Cajon, California.

July 14, 1979 - a George fighter of the 301st Squadron is salvaged from Hido Bay.

The salvaged George was never fully restored. The barnacles were removed and the aircraft was repainted. But all the bullet holes remain.

Bob Applegate in 1987 describing his dogfight with Georges.

LBJ's SILVER STAR - THE MISSION THAT NEVER WAS

by

Barrett Tillman and Henry Sakaida

Lt. Comdr. Lyndon B. Johnson arrives at Seven Mile Drome, Port Moresby, New Guinea, and is greeted by Brig. Gen. Ralph Royce (left) and Brig. Gen. Martin F. Scanlon (shaking hands). Brig. Gen. William H. Marquat, of General MacArthur's staff, who accompanied Johnson, is at far right. (Credit UPI Bettmann)

Lieutenant Commander Lyndon Baines Johnson, a member of the U.S. House of Representatives from Texas temporarily serving in the U.S. Navy, received his nation's third highest combat decoration while on a 1942 fact finding mission. The future president was so proud of his award that he wore the Silver Star lapel pin for the rest of his life.

The Silver Star citation, issued by General Douglas MacArthur's chief of staff, says in part, "While on a mission of obtaining information in the Southwest Pacific Area, Lieutenant Commander Johnson, in order to obtain personal knowledge of combat conditions, volunteered as an observer on a hazardous aerial combat mission over hostile positions in New Guinea. As our planes neared the target area, they were intercepted by eight hostile fighters. When at this time the plane in which Lieutenant Commander Johnson was an observer developed mechanical trouble and was forced to turn back alone, presenting a favorable target to the enemy fighters, he evidenced marked coolness in spite of the hazard involved. His gallant action enabled him to obtain and return with valuable information."

LBJ biographer Robert Caro's **Means of Ascent** takes umbrage at Johnson's receiving the nation's third highest combat medal for what amounted to taking an airplane ride and spending "a few minutes under fire". But even that description overstates the event. The fact is, LBJ never got within sight of Japanese forces. His combat experience was a myth.

The mission of June 9, 1942 was code-named "Tow Nine". It involved eleven Martin B-26 Marauders, fast, twin-engined bombers of the 22nd Bomb Group from Port Moresby, New Guinea. Their target was Lae Aerodrome, an important Japanese installation on New Guinea's Northern coast. Diversionary attacks by B-25 Mitchell and B-17 Flying Fortress bombers were to cover the 22nd's approach. (See map, pg. 90)

Johnson's party arrived by B-17 from Townsville, Queensland, Australia early that morning. But not early enough to prevent a delay in the mission departure. Recalls Noel A. Wright, flying in B-26 No. 40-1496, "Our scheduled departure was delayed, due to the late arrival of expected VIP passengers we were to carry ... by about an hour. I remember the General [Marquat] climbing aboard my airplane [Lieutenant Robert R. Hatch's crew]...the VIP's late arrival at Port Moresby messed up a potentially good raid, cost lives and aircraft..."

LBJ was first assigned to a B-26 named WABASH CANNONBALL, but he apparently left the bomber to retrieve his camera. When he returned, he found his seat taken by Lieutenant Colonel Francis R. Stevens, accompanying Johnson on the tour of the forward area. Stevens playfully told Johnson to find another airplane, so LBJ climbed into Lieutenant Walter H. Greer's 40-1488, named HECKLING HARE (also known to the crew as ARKANSAS TRAVELER).

Takeoff from Port Moresby was at 0851 with First Lieutenant Walter A. Krell leading. The formation arrived over the target area at 1002, by which time only ten B-26s remained. One, the HECKLING HARE, had aborted a half hour after takeoff and returned to base at 1008.

Generator trouble had forced Greer's crew to drop its bombs well short of the target and return. HECKLING HARE had never gotten within sight of Lae.

When the rest of the Marauders returned, it was obvious there had been trouble. One aircraft crash-landed, four more had battle damage, and one never returned at all. The missing plane was the WABASH CANNONBALL. Its entire eight man crew was dead, shot down in the sea off Lae.

Lieutenant Walter A. Krell led the B-26 strike against Lae Airfield on June 9, 1942, (W.A. Krell)

Lt. Col. Francis R. Stevens in a photo taken about a year before he was killed. (F.R. Stevens Jr.)

Lyndon Johnson returned to Townsville the next day, conferred with MacArthur on the 18th, and began the long trip home. He took with him his citation for the Silver Star.

The discrepancy is hard enough to understand on the face of the known facts. But equally surprising is the fact that General Marquat, who lauded Johnson in a personal letter ("you surely earned your decoration") flew in another B-26 on Tow Nine. Was Marquat that obtuse or that sycophantic?

Lyndon Johnson kept a diary during his tour. His entry for the June 9th mission is laconic, "After we were off the field with Prell (sic) and Greer leading, Greer's generator went out: crew begged him to go on. For the next thirty minutes we flew on one generator." There was no mention of combat nor enemy interceptors.

The great LBJ combat myth was born with the publication of **The Mission** in 1964, by Martin Caidin and Edward Hymoff. Caidin was already an established aviation writer, best known for books on space exploration and WWII in the Pacific. He was familiar with Japanese subjects, having previously collaborated with former Imperial Navy officers and Japan's top living fighter ace, Saburo Sakai.

A B-26 Marauder of the 22nd Bomb Group flies over New Guinea. (W.A. Krell)

At this juncture, the Johnson story merges with Sakai's, leading to Caidin and Hymoff's version. For one of the Zero pilots defending Lae against the 22nd Bomb Group was then Flight Petty Officer Saburo Sakai, an accomplished fighter ace who had already destroyed or damaged more than fifty Allied aircraft.

Some two dozen Mitsubishi A6M2 Zeros of the Lae Wing intercepted the remaining ten B-26s moments after the B-25s and B-17s had struck. In fact, inbound Marauders almost collided with the outbound Mitchells - a residual of the Johnson party's late arrival at Port Moresby. The VIP's participation therefore upset a well conceived plan that would have achieved a coordinated attack. **The Mission** was correct in several aspects, however, including the fact that Sakai engaged the Marauders and shot down one. He was credited with two, but his second victim limped back. The Japanese claimed a total of four B-26s shot down. Bomber gunners claimed two Zeroes, but the only Japanese casualty was Petty Officer First Class Sakio Kikuchi.

Let's examine a few of the factors on which the widely spread story hangs. The most dramatic feature is the peril of the HECKLING HARE, allegedly limping from the target with one of its two engines either malfunctioning or shut down - which is unclear. **The Mission** describes a running gunfight with the disabled bomber under attack by perhaps eight Japanese fighters. Could a single-engine B-26 evade the speedy Zeros? An April 1990 phone call to Sakai brought this reaction, "On a clear day? Definitely not! The only chance would be to hide in clouds."

Former B-26 pilots agree, stating that the Marauder's best single engine speed was perhaps 160 mph - far below the Zero's 330. Staff Sergeant Albert Tyree, who flew on this mission, comments on the generator problem. "The electrical system on the early B-26 was marginal to say the least. The system was 12 volt (Greer's ship) but was later converted to the standard 24 volt system. Of course, with the loss of a generator, the turret operation was a concern. However, the major problem was with the Curtiss electric propellers. With only one overloaded generator the possibility of its loss could be critical. With no control and a continuous drop in propeller RPM over a period of time, a landing would be imperative as soon as possible." He further adds, "Nice to hear about LBJ's 'marked coolness and gallant action.' Ha!"

The mathematics of the flight prove that the HARE never reached the target area. The formation took off from Port Moresby at 0851 and Johnson's plane landed an hour and seventeen minutes later, at 1008. Assuming that aircrew statements in **The Mission** are correct, the B-26s cruised at 190 mph. Therefore, the HARE could only have flown some forty minutes before turning back to land at 1008. Even ignoring the reduced airspeed for climbout after takeoff, that puts Johnson no more than 120 miles from base when his plane aborted. At that point, the formation was some eighty miles southwest of Lae and almost that far from the spot the Zeroes intercepted the Marauders after chasing the outbound Mitchells.

According to two crewmen's statements in **The Mission**, old number 1488 was shot to pieces by 20 mm cannon and 7.7 mm machine gun fire. Yet the official mission report, which describes battle damage to five other returning bombers, makes no mention of any damage to the HECKLING HARE.

Further evidence comes from Albert Tyree, a gunner in Marauder 1536. He states, "I remember this mission very well and I recall seeing a B-26 fly out of formation and turn back...I know it wasn't 1363 (First Lieutenant Powell's aircraft) because they had belly landed just before we got back to Port Moresby. We didn't get attacked until the HECKLING HARE had turned around."

Despite its faults, **The Mission** was well received. It could hardly have missed, featuring a perilous flight by a future president in aerial combat with a top enemy fighter ace. In many ways it rivaled John F. Kennedy's saga in PT-109, without the hindrance of official confirmation. Upon publication Caidin and Hymoff sent copies to the White House and received gracious replies from not only Johnson but from Lady Bird and Lynda as well.

Though **The Mission** was riddled with errors, the authors admittedly were handicapped by incomplete documentation (the mission report was unavailable in the U.S.), and by official silence from the White House and the Air Force. According to at least one source, Johnson was "paranoid about Caidin and Hymoff's intention", especially in an election year.

But perhaps most misleading was outright fabrication by two crewmen of the HECKLING HARE (both now deceased). Whole conversations were manufactured by a gunner described by squadronmates as, "a great one for trying to get into the limelight".

In 1964 another participant, a known Democratic activist, was prepared to testify to Johnson's alleged "coolness under fire" and tried to capitalize on their brief wartime acquaintance by inviting the President to a veteran's reunion.

But others were willing to address the facts. The navigator in 40-1480. Second Lieutenant George B. Wallace, said, "The account by Martin Caidin was not 100% accurate, but I'd rather leave the details about 1488 to those that were aboard."

Other fliers also expressed frustration. Lieutenant Raymond Flanagan, the HARE's regular co-pilot, stayed on the ground June 9th replaced by Australian Sergeant-Pilot G.A. McMullin. Four decades later, Flanagan lamented, "If you ever find out what happened on that damned mission I would like to know."

The officer who did know felt it discretionary not to respond. HECKLING HARE's navigator, Second Lieutenant Billy B. Boothe, was the senior crewman to survive the war since the pilot and co-pilot were both killed in later operations. However, Boothe was still on active duty when Caidin and Hymoff researched their book, and required Air Force approval to discuss **The Mission**. Stationed at Ramstein, West Germany, Boothe contacted the Department of the Air Force in Washington, D.C., explaining his situation. He recalls, "They said if I couldn't concur [with Caidin's description] I shouldn't comment either way about it." He retired as a Lieutenant Colonel and despite a cheerful, extroverted nature, continued refusing to discuss the events of June 9, 1942 until 1990. Then breaking his lengthy silence he said, "I kept a secret a long, long time, but then, I'm getting too old. I wanted our [22nd Bomb Group] history to show the facts."

Boothe does not recall exactly when the HECKLING HARE aborted the flight, but says the Marauder never reached sight of Lae. "You got disgusted when you had to turn back," he explained. "We armed our own airplanes, we were so short-handed. All that work wasted."

Clearly, the perception of Johnson's valor as characterized in General Marquat's letter was not shared by the aircrews at the sharp end. Far from the "suicide mission" the general alluded to, the 22nd Bomb Group airmen had a far calmer attitude toward Lae. As attested

Pilots of the Tainan Kokutai on June 9, 1942. This photo was taken just minutes before they scrambled against incoming B-25s and B-26s. Front row, left to right: Petty Officer Third Class Sadao Uehara, unidentified, Leading Airman Yamamoto, and Leading Airman Keisaku Yoshimura. Top, left to right: Petty Officer First Class Saburo Sakai, Petty Officer Third Class Seiji Ishikawa, war correspondent Hajime Yoshida, and unidentified. (Maru)

America's third highest award for valor, the Silver Star, is shown above. As Congressman and President, LBJ was always seen wearing the lapel pin for the Silver Star, as in the portrait below.

by records and combat veterans, the Group lost twice as many aircraft over Rabaul, the naval air bastion on New Britain, as at Lae. Recalled retired Colonel Leon G. Lewis, who flew with Lieutenant Hayes in SHAMROCK, "The targets, Lae and Salamaua, were milk runs; on the other hand, Rabaul was a tough mission. We were not aware at the time of Lyndon Johnson's write-up for the Silver Star; they were scarce for the aircrews."

The exact origins of the contrived decoration to Johnson remain unknown. Major General R.K. Sutherland, MacArthur's chief of staff, made the award in MacArthur's name on June 18, 1942, just nine days after the alleged episode. The following day Brigadier General William F. Marquat wrote Johnson, filling LBJ's request for a signed copy of the citation. In his cover letter, Marquat stated, "Of course, your outstanding bravery in volunteering for a so-called 'suicide mission' in order to get a first hand view of what our Army fliers go through has been the subject of much favorable comment since your departure. It is indeed a great government we have when members of Congress take THOSE chances in order to better serve their fellow men in the legislative bodies. You surely earned you decoration and I am so happy about your having received the award."

The decoration remains a sore point with many 22nd Bomb Group veterans. The HARE's crew chief, retired Master Sergeant Woodrow W. Harrison said, "As to the strangeness of LBJ's Silver Star ... no other crew member aboard 1488 received one."

Equally adamant was the HARE's regular gunner, Robert Marshall, who said, "We didn't know (LBJ) was awarded the Silver Star until the book came out. We didn't like it. If he got it, then so should everyone else on the mission."

In truth, if any decoration was awarded the various observers on the mission, it should have been the Air Medal. Ordinarily presented for five or more missions, it was regarded by aviators as an "I was there" award. It served as a means of setting apart those who have performed a combat function. The award of the Silver Star - even had Johnson's citation been accurate - was an insult to every man who earned the medal.

How, then, was the nation's third highest award for valor presented literally for taking an airplane ride? Robert Caro indicates the decoration originated with Douglas MacArthur himself, since he authorized Lieutenant Colonel Steven's posthumous Distinguished Service Cross - second only to the Medal of Honor. After all, MacArthur held the "Congressional" for little more than taking a boat ride when President Roosevelt ordered him out of the Philippines. By some accounts, the general coveted the medal since his father had won it in the Civil War. Given that background, was MacArthur contemptuous of lesser decorations? Or was he pandering to a well connected congressman in an attempt to curry political favor? The Pacific Theater was the poor cousin of America's war effort until late 1943. MacArthur may simply have been trying to gain more influence for his area of operations.

A postscript to **The Mission** does contain a bittersweet element. In a 1987 airshow at Yakima, Washington, former Zero pilot Saburo Sakai was an honored guest with several American aces and, although lacking English, graciously received well wishers and autograph seekers. Among the curious Americans was the son of Lieutenant Colonel Francis Stevens, who had died under Sakai's guns in WABASH CANNONBALL some forty-four years before.* With the help of a translator, Sakai and F.R. Stevens Jr. (retired USAF colonel) discussed the events of the June 9th mission.

However, combat veterans of a much later war seem in wide agreement that on June 9, 1942, Petty Officer Saburo Sakai never got a shot at Congressman Lyndon Baines Johnson.

*Although Sakai claimed two B-26s on this mission, only one was lost (Second Lieutenant Willis Bench's #1508). According to Second Lieutenant Dewey C. Flint, "I was flying on Bench's wing, the formation was too close, too low. Bench got dragged into the water. I saw the whole thing." Bench's aircraft was apparently flying OK and was not in trouble when he went in.

Albert Tyree and Saburo Sakai crossed paths on June 9, 1942. They cement their new friendship with a handshake in San Jose, California in 1991. (Al Tyree)

Saburo Sakai at the Stevens home near Yakima. Stevens is holding Sakai's torn flight helmet, the one he wore when cricaly wounded in combat over the Solomons.

THE MASTER FALCON

Lieutenant Hinoki with an early model Oscar, 1942. (Hinoki)

In the "Forgotten Campaign" of the China-Burma-India theater of operations, outstanding fighter leaders not only battled the enemy, but also their high command for a share of scarce equipment, supplies and reinforcement. With the great battles being waged in the Pacific and Europe, the CBI was given low priority on both sides. Even today more than forty-five years after the end of World War II, very little is known about the men who flew against our pilots in this vast area. Here is the story of Yohei Hinoki, one of the great fighter pilots of the Japanese Army Air Force and some of those he encountered.

Hinoki was born in 1919. He received his flight commission in June 1941 and joined the Army's illustrious 64th Sentai in November. Captain Iwori Sakai, an accomplished technician with over nine victories in the Nomohan (Khalkin Gol) and Manchurian air battles, taught the young shavetail the finer points of dogfighting. Sakai was so impressed with his subordinate's abilities that he presented him with his own custom made flight helmet.. Hinoki would wear it until the end of the war.

The Japanese launched the Pacific War on December 8, 1941 with simultaneous strikes against Pearl Harbor, the Philippines, Hong Kong, and Malaya. The 64th Sentai, led by its legendary leader Major (later Major General) Tateo Kato, attacked British and Commonwealth Forces in support of the invasion force over Malaya. The Malayan Campaign which resulted in the capture of strategic Singapore, Britain's chief naval base in the Far East, took only fifty-four days.

Major Tateo Kato led the 64th Sentai from April 1941 until he was killed in May 1942. He was a great fighter/leader who scored over 18 victories. The 64th Sentai became the most famous JAAF unit during WWII

Brewster F2A Buffalo; it was aptly named and suffered the same fate as its namesake. (Trevor Coker)

Lieutenant Hinoki was assigned as Major Kato's wingman. Kato led eighteen aircraft against the British over Kuala Lumpur on December 22, 1941. In the unit's first dogfight of the new war, they claimed eleven Brewster F2A Buffaloes. The enemy aircraft was aptly named and suffered the same fate as their namesake. Two RAF Hurricanes from 258 Squadron went down before Hinoki's guns on January 31, 1942 over Singapore.

The 64th Sentai was equipped with the Ki-43 Hayabusa (Peregrine Falcon). A workhorse of the Japanese Army Air Force, it was given the Allied code name "Oscar". A featherweight in terms of armament, it sported only two nose-mounted 12.7mm machine guns. Maximum speed was 320 mph at 13,125 feet. Although lacking sufficient firepower, this was more than compensated for by its extreme maneuverability. In the hands of a skilled pilot like Hinoki, the Oscar became a formidable weapon.

It was inevitable that the famed American Volunteer Group, "Flying Tigers", would clash head-on with the 64th Sentai as it ventured forward. Lieutenant Hinoki's April 10, 1942 encounter with the Americans nearly cost him his life. Major Kato led his men to attack Loiwing Airfield at 0610, just across the border from Burma. Their first strike did little damage. They came back in the afternoon for a knock out blow, but this time the Flying Tigers were waiting for them.

Lieutenant Hinoki spotted four P-40s coming toward him. "They must be well trained and experienced pilots," he thought. "They must be very furious about our early morning attack." As the P-40s dove on Lieutenant Takeshi Endo's flight, Hinoki reacted by firing on them. Apparently caught by surprise, two of the Americans dove away with Hinoki on their tail.

In a dangerous low level dogfight in the clouds, Hinoki traded fire with Flight Lieutenant Robert T. Smith of the 3rd AVG Squadron. Suddenly as he came out of the last big cloud, Hinoki saw a P-40 slightly below him and prepared to shoot. As he fired he heard the sound of bullets hitting his own plane. The gauges on his instrument panel exploded. He felt a severe shock on his left arm and buttocks. Blood covered his face. "When I looked at the right wing, I could see a vapor trail of leaking fuel," he recalls. He had taken twenty-one hits.

Unable to think clearly Hinoki made a spontaneous decision to destroy himself by crashing his fighter into a mountain peak but regained his senses, as the fuel leak stopped. Then he spotted a familiar river landmark and decided that he wanted to live. Hinoki had lost precious gasoline and he had no idea how much he had left. In an agonizing two hour flight home he reached an airfield in Thailand and glided in, having exhausted his fuel. His parachute harness had stopped one of R.T.'s .50 caliber slugs from entering his back just above his heart. The surgeon removed another bullet from his left upper arm which he would keep as a souvenir for the rest of his life, but he could not remove one from his buttocks. Hinoki had his wings "clipped" and spent over a month in the hospital.

R.T. Smith claimed an Oscar destroyed and one probable (Hinoki). He did not know the name of his

Flying Tiger Ace, Flight Leader R.T. Smith, 3rd AVG Squadron, circa 1942 in his P-40B. Hinoki's encounter with R.T. nearly cost him his life, but he managed to struggle home. (R.T. Smith)

opponents of that day until informed in 1991. "I wish I could have met Hinoki," said the old Tiger. "We would have had a lot to talk about."

Hinoki returned to Japan and became an instructor with the Akeno Army Fighter School but was reassigned to his old unit in Burma in March 1943. Two months later he was made a company commander and participated in the air defense of Rangoon. RAF Hurricanes and Mohawks were the main opponents over Burma during this time, but the equation was about to change for the worse with the introduction of the P-51 Mustang.

The P-51 Mustang made its combat debut over the CBI with the arrival of the 311th Fighter-Bomber Group. The unit was activated in 1942 and was untested in combat. Their P-51As and A-36s (dive bomber version) arrived in India to support Allied ground forces in Northern Burma. The leader of the group was Colonel Harry Ripley Melton, Jr.

"Rip" Melton was born in Kentucky in 1911. His father, Major (later General) Harry R. Melton, was in the Army Medical Corps. An only son, he graduated from West Point in 1936 and entered the Air Corps receiving flight training at Randolph and Kelly Fields in Texas. After serving as commander of the 84th Bomb Group in Georgia, he took command of the 311th Fighter Bomber Group on

Colonel Tateo Kato and his Oscar over Burma. (Depiction by Shori Tanaka)

November 26, 1942. Colonel Melton took his unit to India via Australia in July 1943.

Aloysius X. Hiltgen, a member of the 311th (530th Fighter Squadron), fondly recalls this dynamic leader:

"Colonel Harry 'Rip' Melton was admired and respected by every member of the group. The nickname 'Rip' came from the expression, 'He would rip you a new ___' if you screwed up. I was on the receiving end of this a number of times and I deserved every one. He made me write, 'I will not violate flying regulations', 500 times a day for two weeks for obvious reason but then protected me from higher ups who wanted me court martialled. He was a helluva man. His wife, Natalie, was a very attractive woman with a great deal of charm."

November 25,1943 marked the first duel between Mustangs of the 311th and Oscars of the 64th. There were two missions flown by the 311th that day. The first resulted in two victories and a loss. The second mission, escorting a dozen B-25s of the 490th Bomb Squadron to Mingaladon, was led by the "old man" himself.

The Mitchells bombed under a 7,000 foot overcast and hit airfield installations and damaged two aircraft. They were intercepted by twelve Oscars from the 64th Sentai and five twin-engined escort fighters (Nicks) from the 21st Sentai. Second Lieutenant Clifton L. Bray attacked one of the Nicks at 8,000 feet, closed to point blank range and exploded the left engine. The enemy aircraft spiraled to the left and dove all the way to the ground. The pilot of the Nick was Corporal Seito Takahashi of the 21st Sentai.

The 64th Sentai had been alerted to meet the attack and Lieutenant Hinoki, scrambled with three others from the 3rd Squadron. After takeoff his radio failed and he prepared to land when he caught sight of seven unfamiliar aircraft at much higher altitude. Retracting his landing gear, he led his flight to investigate. At first he thought it was a formation of twin-engined Nicks, the large wing drop tanks looking like twin engines from a distance, but they were, in fact, the 311th Group's P-51s.

Hinoki didn't have a good feeling about the bogies. The Japanese made their approach with the sun behind them. The still unidentified aircraft had a 1,000 foot altitude advantage. Hinoki rocked his wings in a friendly gesture and at that moment, Colonel Melton returned the salutation with a burst of gunfire. Simultaneously, Lieutenant Goichi Sumino returned fire.

Melton's rude response startled Hinoki. Bullets punctured his wing, but the damage was minor. Before Hinoki could react, the Mustangs flashed past. Looking over his shoulder, he saw the large white USAAF star on the wings.

Hinoki turned onto the tail of the American leader who executed a "Split-S" maneuver, exposing his underside. It was a fatal mistake. Hinoki recalls this moment:

"Colonel Melton made the mistake of flipping his Mustang over. If he had dived away to the left or right without exposing his belly, I'm sure he could have escaped. I got a clear shot at him from close range and gave him a burst from my guns. I knew I got him because chunks of metal and smoke came spewing out. I made just one firing pass on his fighter before breaking off to help my comrades."

Harry R. Melton Jr., West Point Class of 1936.

The aerial sparring soon turned into a bloody slugfest. Melton's wingman nearly got the best of Hinoki, but luckily Warrant Officer Kinoshita charged in to save him. Kinoshita latched on and pursued the American doggedly for over a hundred miles. He reported that he had shot down the enemy into a river. Lieutenant Sumino was under attack and the duel reached zero altitude. He returned to base and reported that he sent his victim down into the sea.

It wasn't until Hinoki's men had all landed that they realized that their opponents had been the new P-51.

Second Lieutenant Clifton L. Bray of the 530th Fighter Squadron "Yellow Scorpions" claimed a "Nick" on November 25, 1943.

Lieutenant Yohei Hinoki poses on the wing of his Oscar. Army pilots sometimes carried their swords in their cockpit for good luck. (Hinoki)

They were favorably impressed. Although the Japanese had made a number of claims, only one Mustang was lost - the aircraft flown by Colonel Harry Melton. One Mustang was lost on an earlier mission and two others sustained damages. "We didn't lose any fighters," recalls Hinoki, "but I knew the P-51s were going to be really troublesome from then on."

Melton had suffered hits in the cooling system. Captain Sidney M. Newcomb related:

"Colonel Melton and I had left the target area (Rangoon) approximately 1310 hours, 25 November 1943 and the Colonel was flying at full speed. His speed began to drop progressively some distance out from the target and it became necessary for me to throttle back in order to stay with him. The Colonel asked me over the radio to throttle back further still but I was unable to do so and maintain my flying speed. I called Colonel Melton over the radio to ask what was wrong. He did not give me his trouble, but told me to head home and not circle. At this point, a trail of black smoke appeared out of the exhaust on the Colonel's ship. I saw him slide back his canopy and bail out approximately 1,000 feet above the trees. He waved to me after his parachute had opened. His ship crashed about one half mile away and exploded. Upon landing the Colonel's parachute disappeared among the trees. I circled the spot several times but saw no more of him. I then proceeded on my course and landed at Ramu."

Tenth Air Force conducted an all-out search for the missing group commander without success. Melton had bailed out about 100 miles northwest of Rangoon and about twenty miles east of the Bay of Bengal and was captured almost immediately on landing.

Dudley Hogan, another pilot from the same group, was shot down on November 27th and captured two days later near Gwa Bay not too far from where Melton had parachuted. The two airmen were incarcerated together. Hogan was shipped to Rangoon suffering burns to his face and arms. Melton went later, spent about a month in Rangoon undergoing interrogation and very cruel treatment, and was passed on to a POW camp in Singapore. A 26th Fighter Squadron P-40 pilot, Second Lieutenant Walter H. Stiles, met Melton in the Changi POW Camp on June 9, 1944. Stiles survived the war and reported that they were confined together until September 2nd. He stated that Melton was in good spirits, was confident that they would be released soon, and was in as good health as could be expected under the circumstances.

Colonel Melton was the sole American amongst 1,319 British and Australian prisoners being transferred to Japan aboard the transport **Rakuyo Maru** leaving Singapore around September 4th in a convoy carrying oil and raw rubber to Japan. They never made it.

On September 12, 1944 in the South China Sea the convoy ran into an American submarine wolf-pack consisting of the **Sealion** (SS-195), **Growler** (SS-215) and **Pampanito** (SS-383 now on public display at Fisherman's Wharf in San Francisco). The **Sealion** sent a torpedo into the **Rakuyo Maro** at 0530 and it burst into flames. The other POW ship, **Kachidoki Maru**, carrying over 900 prisoners was disabled, rammed a burning tanker and caught fire. Colonel Melton boarded a lifeboat, but his luck was only temporary. The submarines pursued the convoy's surviving ships, not realizing at the time that they had attacked transports loaded with Allied POWs. Three days later all three submarines returned to the scene of the carnage to rescue survivors, but Colonel Melton was not among them.

Prisoners aboard the **Rakuyo Maru** boarded life boats, rafts or clung to floating debris. A survivor reported:

"The prisoners separated into two groups; one consisting of three boats and the other of eight. The group of three sailed westward in an effort to reach the coast of China or Indo-China. On the following morning, they sighted the group of eight boats which was sailing westward, but the groups again became separated that afternoon. When last seen, the group of eight appeared to be heading northeast. During the night one of the boats from the group of eight joined the group of three but the other seven were not in sight. It was later ascertained, from statements of the survivors, that Colonel Melton was with the seven missing boats.

"During the morning, the men in the four boats heard sounds of distant gunfire and shortly afterward, three Japanese destroyers appeared, one of which picked up the men in the four boats. The survivors indicated to the Japanese that there were seven boats in the vicinity and were advised by a Japanese naval officer that they were aware of the fact. The survivors believed that the men had been rescued by the other two destroyers but later found that this was not true."

Colonel Harry R. Melton, Jr. was posthumously awarded the Distinguished Flying Cross for "extraordinary achievement in aerial flight." At the time of his death, he left his wife, Natalie, and their only child, a daughter named Livonia Anne.

Soon after Colonel Melton had been captured Lieutenant Hinoki received a congratulatory telephone call from headquarters. A staff officer told him that the pilot of the Mustang was a full colonel and gave him his name. Hinoki was very surprised to learn that an officer of such high rank had been flying a combat mission.

"I was given the opportunity of meeting Colonel Melton, but I declined to do so," recalls Hinoki.

Two days later on November 27th Lieutenant Hinoki was once again in the midst of heavy action and the 311th would extract revenge for their leader's loss. Hinoki would pay dearly. Bombers returned to demolish the Insein locomotive shops. They were escorted by Mustangs from the 311th and P-38s of the 459th Fighter Squadron. Hinoki describes the initial dogfight with the American fighters:

"There was a formation of five B-24s and above them, four P-51s. OK, you're in for it. I climbed for altitude and got to the rear of the Mustangs. They hadn't spotted me. I closed in and sighted one in my gunsight. I chuckled to myself; it was certainly the enemy. I was confident as I prepared. The distance was 100 meters, then ninety meters, then eighty meters. My machine guns flamed. I hit it. The enemy plane burst into flames and went into a tail spin."

The "Master Falcon" then jumped into another melee - this time with the Lightnings. He went on to flame one. Captain John E. Fouts, Jr., their leader, described the action later in his combat report:

"I was leading a two ship element, four ship flight, escorting a flight of B-24s at an altitude of 20,000 over Rangoon. Captain Ortmeyer, with Lieutenant Harlan as wingman, formed the 2nd element echelon to right. Second Lieutenant James G. Harris was my wingman.

"I saw five Zeros [Oscars were frequently misidentified as Zeros and vice versa] at twelve o'clock, 3000 feet below us. We started down to make a pass and as we did, the Zeros turned away. While diving I looked behind and saw six other Zeros following us. I gave the orders to drop auxiliary tanks and give it the 'gun'. We pulled up in a chandelle trying to get on the tail of the Zeros. The last time I saw Captain Ortmeyer and Lieutenant Harlan was when we started our dive on the five Zeros."

Captain Armin J. Ortmeyer and Second Lieutenant Jay R. Harlan were shot down during this encounter and were never recovered. It is certain that Hinoki downed one of them. With two victories under his belt, he decided to tackle the heavies. He joined up with Lieutenant Shiro Suzuki and pursued the bombers to the coast. Bomber gunners threw a wall of lead at the pair. Suzuki was hit and bailed out, but didn't survive.

"As soon as the bombers hit the coast, their orderly straight line formation went to pieces. Everybody scattered," exclaimed Hinoki. "So, I concentrated on the stragglers and made a total of seven head-on attacks. I dropped two B-24s in this fashion. Then a funny thing

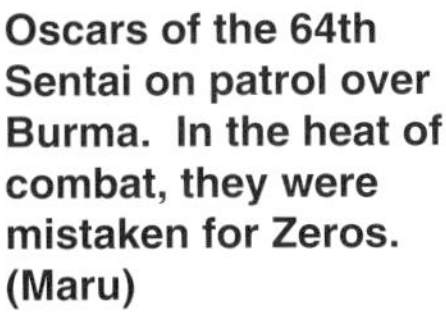

Oscars of the 64th Sentai on patrol over Burma. In the heat of combat, they were mistaken for Zeros. (Maru)

happened. The entire formation of B-24s suddenly made a U-turn and headed straight back towards me! I think they received the SOS signals from the stragglers and came back to help. I couldn't believe it."

The two Liberators that Hinoki downed belonged to the 308th Bomb Group. No. 245 was piloted by Lieutenant R.W. Meredith of the 373rd Squadron. No. 312 was piloted by Second Lieutenant N.J. Kellam of the 374th. The crews were never seen again.

Hinoki's luck also ran out and he recounts what followed:

"Evidently the P-51 escorts heard their SOS signal because without warning and almost out of nowhere, I got hit. A Mustang came up from below in a climbing firing pass, turned around, and made a dive to finish me off. My plane spun out of control, no smoke or fire. That guy had hit everything but my engine. I got a .50 caliber bullet through my right leg. There was blood all over the cockpit and I thought I would pass out because of the excruciating pain. I wrapped my silk scarf in a tourniquet around my spurting leg and somehow managed to land at an air base."

The payback was delivered by Second Lieutenant Robert F. Mulhollem, a member of the 311th's 530th Fighter Squadron. Hinoki's Oscar was one of three that he had hit in the fierce fighting. He received credit for one destroyed and had two probables. (Mulhollen became an ace on May 12, 1944 with his fifth victory.)

It had been a costly mission for the Americans. Losses for the day amounted to four P-51s, three B-24s (one ditched and the crew were rescued), and two P-38s. Bomber gunners claimed thirteen victories and seven probables but the 64th Sentai only lost one plane and pilot.

As a result of this combat, Lieutenant Hinoki lost a part of his right leg and was hospitalized for months. In February 1944 he returned to Japan where he underwent further medical treatment and was fitted with a wooden leg. Because of his invaluable combat experience and burning desire to return to duty, he was assigned to the Akeno Fighter School in November 1944 as an instructor.

Second Lieutenant Robert F. Mulhollem, 530th Fighter Squadron of the 311th Fighter-Bomber Group, in his personal aircraft. (R.F. Mulhollem)

Lieutenant Yohei Hinoki in hospital garb after having his leg amputated as a result of his combat of November 27, 1943.

On July 16, 1945 Field Order No. 146 was issued to the USAAF Seventh Fighter Command based on Iwo Jima. The fighter groups (21st and 506th) had been flying very long range missions to Japan for many weeks. The mission for the day was to strafe airfields in the Nagoya area. Forty-eight Mustangs from the 506th took off just before 1015, led by Major Malcolm C. Watters. They were accompanied by some B-29s for navigation. The Group reached the Japanese mainland shortly before 1330.

The Akeno Fighter School was alerted to enemy aircraft activity and scrambled their aircraft. This was an operational training unit - Japan's "Top Gun" school for Army pilots. It was located at Akeno in Mie Prefecture, directly south across Ise-Wan (Nagoya Bay). The unit was undergoing reorganization to become the 111th Sentai, one of the last to be formed in the war and were equipped with the best Army fighters available - Ki-84 Franks and Ki-100 Goshikisens. Yohei Hinoki, now a major, commanded a twelve plane squadron of Ki-100s.

With the 506th Group's Mustangs heading over Ise-Wan, Major Hinoki placed his squadron above and to the right of Major Toyoki Eto's squadron. The two squadrons flew over to Shinmiya, then turned left and headed down the coast to Shimahanto. Just above the Ise Shrine, at around 21,000 feet, Captain Katsuji Sugiyama, leading the fourth flight in Hinoki's squadron, made a

A lineup of Red Tailed P-51 Mustangs of the 457th Ftr. Sq., 506th Ftr Grp. on Iwo Jima.

sudden right turn toward the ocean. Hinoki followed with his flight and the distance between his and Eto's squadron rapidly increased. Hinoki remembers, "They looked so small, just like long floating strings."

Captain Sugiyama led his flight downward, right into the Mustangs of the 457th and 458th Fighter Squadrons. Major Hinoki had to speed up to stay with them and provide cover. He watched the enemy formation react, making a sudden turn and noticed that there were eleven of them, in flights of four, four, and three. Hinoki approached the last plane in the formation. He was in a vengeful mood as a Mustang had taken his leg over Burma. He noticed that his aircraft was sliding a lot due to a propeller problem when he increased throttle. The Ki-100 Goshikisen had just become operational in March. It was basically a standard Ki-61 Tony airframe with a powerful radial engine. Not all of the "bugs" had been worked out of it.

Major Hinoki dived on the Mustang. "I approached until I could see - so to speak - the enemy pilot's white teeth," he recalls. "Even if my plane skidded, I couldn't miss. I fired from twenty meters and then saw the enemy plane spinning down, as if in its death struggle. I glanced back and there were ten enemy planes behind me."

The Mustang that Hinoki had just hit was piloted by Captain John W. Benbow of the 457th who had been leading the second element in Captain William B. Lawrence's flight. What Benbow was doing in the tail end position is hard to explain. Perhaps Hinoki was mistaken about his location. Captain Lawrence had pulled onto the tail of an enemy aircraft which was making an easy turn to the right at 15,000 feet. Benbow's flight followed it into a "Split S" as the enemy plane began smoking and disintegrating. Benbow had called out over the radio, "That's enough, Bill. You've got him."

Second Lieutenant Joseph D. Winn, Benbow's wingman was flying through so much debris that he was forced to break off briefly and lost Benbow from view.

Captain Benbow was never seen again. At approximately that time and in the same area, an aircraft believed to be a P-51 was seen by another flight in apparent trouble, going down in slow gliding turns at an estimated 150 mph. It disappeared into clouds around 8,000 feet. Yet another flight saw a white parachute in this same area five minutes later.

Major Hinoki found himself alone and under vicious attack. He was forced to make tighter and tighter turns to keep from being hit. Fortunately, the Goshikisen could outturn the nimble Mustangs. Hinoki wanted desperately to withdraw from this uneven combat, but the leader of the P-51s was attacking him in a very aggressive manner. With great confidence in his plane's new HA-112-II engine, Hinoki finally pushed the nose straight down and opened full throttle. He was amazed at how steady his aircraft was, although he could feel and hear the tremendous air pressure. When he finally pulled out of the dive, the enemy had disappeared.

Major Hinoki believed that the Mustangs had intended to attack the Kyuko area, but his unit's intervention had undoubtedly thwarted that plan. When the battle

Ki-100 Goshiki-Sen of the Akeno Fighter School. This was flown by First Lieutenant Mamoru Tatsuda of Hinoki's squadron on the July 16, 1945 skirmish. (Hinoki)

ended, the Goshikisen pilots made claims of six Mustangs shot down with five probables. Actually, only four P-51s were hit and Captain John W. Benbow was the only casualty from the 506th Fighter Group. Akeno Fighter School lost five aircraft and three pilots (Captain Motomichi Suzuki and First Lieutenants Jiro Oka and Eijo Takano). The Seventh Fighter Command claimed twenty-five victories, two probables, and eighteen damaged for their day's work.

The Akeno Fighter School was very proud to have shown their colors. After the July 16th skirmish, it was transformed into the 111th Sentai. However, the war was nearing the end and the unit saw no further action of any significance. As for Japan's most famous "One Legged Ace", Major Hinoki ended his flying career in Hyogo Prefecture. In home defense, he flew missions against B-29s and their escorts. He had scored at least twelve confirmed aerial victories during the war, a remarkable record for any Japanese fighter pilot flying against the Americans and the British.

In October 1980, Yohei Hinoki, a Tokyo resident, learned for the first time about the fate of the USAAF colonel that he had shot down over Burma some thirty-six years prior. Major General Charles Chandler of Santa Cruz, California (now deceased) had been a close friend of Melton's. In a letter dated October 3, 1980, Chandler writes:

Hinoki describes his encounter with Colonel Harry R. Melton Jr. in 1980

"Colonel Melton did not survive the war. After he was captured and held as a war criminal in Rangoon, he was moved to Singapore. From Singapore, he, with many other Allied prisoners of war, was in the process of being moved to Japan by transport. They were torpedoed by an American submarine. However, the transport sank slowly enough to enable all personnel aboard to evacuate to life boats. Prisoners were loaded in life boats separately from the transport's crew, with one exception - a British officer, who for some reason was loaded with the crew. Japanese destroyers then sank all of the prisoners' life boats. The sole survivor was the British officer, and he was the person who confirmed Colonel Melton's death to the War Department. This same officer also wrote to Colonel Melton's wife, giving her all the details. He also enclosed a love letter that Colonel Melton had written to his wife while in Singapore. The British officer carried the letter between the insole and sole of his shoe until the war's end. Believe it or not, this letter was still legible except where folded."

The discovery of Colonel Melton's tragic fate stunned Hinoki. For several moments he was speechless and lost in deep thought. Then he sighed, "I'm truly saddened and sorry to hear this. It's such a shame he died in that manner."

In June 1986 Mr. Hinoki wrote a letter to Natalie Melton which was translated into English and forwarded. In the letter he described his combat with her husband: "I made three big holes in his plane, but he skillfully evaded me. I know that I did not hurt him." Hinoki ended his letter with, "I heard that your husband died en route to Japan - it was so regrettable. You must be strong and live."

Tokyo, 1980. Mr. Hinoki presents the author with his custom-made flight helmet. In this meeting, he was told about the fate of Colonel Harry R. Melton Jr.

The common expression "It's a small world" can certainly apply to Hinoki. His son runs the popular Taiko Japanese Restaurant in Irvine, California. He is usually behind the sushi bar and greets all visitors. By strange coincidence, General Charles Chandler's son, a police lieutenant had dined at Taiko without ever suspecting the war-time connection. Chandler had assumed command of the 311th Fighter Bomber Group when Colonel Harry R. Melton was lost. Robert F. Mulhollem, who seriously wounded Hinoki and took his leg, lived not more than twenty miles from the restaurant. He became an airline pilot after the war and was living in retirement by 1981.

Yohei Hinoki became a successful businessman after the war and wrote about his war experiences. His memoir, **Tsubasa No Kessen** (Wings of Bloody Combat) was published in Japan in 1976 and became a best seller. He was active in the affairs of the 64th Sentai Association and his name became synonymous with "Kato Hayabusa Sentoki Tai" (Hayabusa Fighter Group Kato).

For many years Mr. Hinoki was a familiar sight in Koganei City (Tokyo) where he could be seen riding his bicycle daily. The "Master Falcon" passed away on January 29, 1991 at age seventy.

Among his ashes Mrs. Hinoki found a bullet fired by Flying Tiger ace, R.T. Smith, forty-eight years earlier. His artificial leg and other items were donated to the Shuubudai Memorial Center at Irima Air Base of the Japan Self Defense Air Force and there the spirit of the "Master Falcon" lives on.

R.T. Smith today, examines Hinoki's flight helmet which he was wearing when R.T. wounded him over Loiwing, China on April 10, 1942

Hinoki (left) poses with his crew chief under his Oscar in 1943. (Hinoki)

A COUNTRY BOY FROM NIIGATA PREFECTURE

Shoichi Sugita was a lot like our American "Ace of Aces" - Dick Bong. Both were country boys with a penchant for flying. They mastered the art of dogfighting and went on to become great aces. Both started their combat career in 1942 and both were killed in 1945.

Born in a remote mountain village of Western Honshu in Niigata Prefecture on July 1, 1924, his early life was full of hardships due to the poverty and harsh climate of the area. Military service offered the only way to escape from the drudgery of farm life so he dropped out of school and enlisted in the navy in 1940.

The flight training program, prior to heavy attrition suffered in the disaster at Midway, June 1942, was very comprehensive. Training went far beyond the fundamentals to include such skills as navigation and packing parachutes. Sugita graduated from flight school in March 1942 and was one of the last group of pilots to have received quality training. Despite this, more than ninety per cent of his classmates did not survive the war.

Tsukuba Air Base, May 1941. Student pilot Shoichi Sugita standing on right. Standing next to him is Takeo Tanimizu, who went on to score over thirty-two victories and survived the war. (T.Tanimizu)

Sugita was assigned to the 6th Kokutai shortly before the Battle of Midway but he did not see combat. All of his unit's aircraft were lost in battle and its surviving pilots sent back to Japan. Sugita arrived in Rabaul in October 1942 aboard the carrier **Zuiho** and became a member of the 204th Kokutai the following month.

Very much like our top ace Dick Bong, Sugita was good from the start. On December 1, 1942, he claimed his first aerial victory when he reportedly attacked, then rammed a B-17 over Buin, Bougainville tearing off a part of his right wing. A good natured fellow with a rustic personality, he soon became known for his aggressiveness in combat. He would often tell his comrades, "Whenever I see an enemy I go after him, no matter what."

In April 1943 the Americans intercepted and successfully decoded a Japanese radio message giving details of Admiral Isoroku Yamamoto's special inspection tour of the Solomon Islands. This set the stage for one of the most famous combat missions ever flown. The decoded message read, "Commander in Chief, Combined Fleet will personally inspect Ballale, Shortland and Buin on April 18th." (See map, pg. 91)

Shoichi Sugita was one of six Zero pilots selected to escort the two Betty bombers carrying the Admiral and his staff. The escort pilots were little more than teenagers - Sugita himself was only eighteen and the rest were not much older. The escorts, in two flights of three each, consisted of the leader, Lieutenant (jg) Takeshi Morizaki, with Petty Officer First Class Toyomitsu Tsujinoue and Flight Leading Seaman Shoichi Sugita. The second flight consisted of Chief Petty Officer Yoshimi Hidaka, Petty Officer Second Class Yasuji Okazaki and Flight Leading Seaman Kenji Yanagiya.

The P-38 ambush party, composed of pilots from the 70th and 339th Fighter Squadrons, departed Fighter Two Airstrip on Guadalcanal. They were led by Major John W. Mitchell. The sixteen P-38s arrived at the killing zone on the southwest coast of Bougainville after flying more than 400 miles over a circuitous all-water route, altitude ranging from ten to thirty feet. The timing was near perfect. Admiral Yamamoto was known for his strict punctuality. It was 0934 when First Lieutenant Doug Canning broke radio silence. "Bogey's eleven o'clock."

First Lieutenant Rex T. Barber and Captain Thomas G. Lanphier Jr. went after the pair of bombers while Major Mitchell took his men up to cover the killing team. Chief Petty Officer Hidaka spotted the P-38s but since they had no radios in their aircraft, they could not effectively communicate with the bombers. Probably no

The Yamamoto Escort Flight

Takeshi Morizaki

Yoshimi Hidaka

Toyomitsu Tsujinoue

Yasuji Okazaki

Shoichi Sugita

Kenji Yanagiya

(Credit: Maru and Yanagiya)

one in the bombers knew that an attack was under way until bullets from Barber's P-38 were slamming into the lead aircraft. Warrant Officer Takeo Kotani, piloting Yamamoto's bomber, gunned his engines and dove while the second Betty tried to follow. The Zeros released their drop tanks and pulled ahead to run interference, but the attack was so sudden they had no chance to mount an effective defense.

Lieutenant (j.g.) Morizaki led his flight in a desperate head-on attack against Lanphier's lead P-38. Reacting to the menace, Lanphier temporarily abandoned pursuit of the Bettys and exchanged fire with the Zeros, later claiming that as a result of his shooting one of the Japanese fighters lost a wing and twisted out of sight on fire and smoking. But none of Morizaki's flight were hit in the initial exchange, and by this time Barber and Holmes had dispatched the two bombers, the lead aircraft carrying Yamamoto to his death.

Barber recalls details of the event: "The bombers were still in formation and on course toward Ballale when the three Zeros dove on us. Lanphier's going for the Zeros was a wise move on his part, as it allowed me the opportunity to attack the bombers without momentary concern of Zeros on my tail."

Barber positioned himself on the lead bomber's tail and started directing his fire from fifty yards. Chunks of metal came flying off the right engine with black smoke. He fired into the wing root, then the fuselage and left engine. The Betty snapped to the left with Barber tailgating less than 100 feet behind and level, pouring his fire into the crippled bomber. Barber nearly struck the bomber's right wing as he flashed past. The shoot down of Admiral Yamamoto's bomber, from the first shot to the crash, was less than thirty seconds.

With Morizaki taking on Lanphier, Tsujinoue picked out First Lieutenant Besby F. Holmes. He noted in his report that the P-38 had failed to release its drop tank. This was definitely Holmes. He fired on Holmes and noted a thin plume of white vapor streaming out. Thinking that he had scored fatal hits, he let it go to protect the Bettys. Sugita directed his attack on First Lieutenant Raymond K. Hine.

Sugita fired on Hine and reported black smoke coming from one of its engines. Suddenly, another Lightening dove on him and he received hits in his engine. Instinctively, Sugita whipped his fighter around and counterattacked, claiming hits in the wing root. The dogfight continued, but the P-38s had already accomplished their objective.

The two Betty bombers were downed almost immediately and the facts surrounding this combat have remained in heated controversy ever since. Although Captain Lanphier has claimed sole credit for the destruction of Admiral Yamamoto's bomber, his contention cannot be supported in the light of new evidence. Those who argue that the "truth will never be known" fail to realize that the Yamamoto Mission is not ancient history. It occurred less than fifty years ago. The key evidence is still lying there on the floor of the jungle.

Captain Lanphier has claimed that he had hit the lead bomber broadside from extreme range after rolling up and diving away from the Zeros. He claimed to have shot the right wing off of Yamamoto's bomber and that the tail gunner was firing at him. Inspection of the wreck revealed that the right wing is lying near the bomber. It had not been shot off during flight. Additionally, there was no evidence of a tail gun. With Zeros hot on his tail, he simply did not have the time nor the opportunity to get at the bombers.

"Rendezvous Over Bougainville", 1988 by Shigeo Koike, depicts the downing of Admiral Yamamoto. First Lieutenant Rex Barber in Miss Virginia passes the stricken bomber while Captain Tom Lanphier (background) draws the Zero escorts away from Barber. (Gene Monihan)

First Lieutenant Raymond K. Hine, the only American casualty on the Yamamoto Mission.

Lieutenant Rex Barber attacked Yamamoto's bomber. His account is consistent with the new findings whereas Lanphier's is not. Kenji Yanagiya, the sole escort pilot to survive the war, confirmed the attack by Barber in a 1975 Tokyo interview. He stated that he saw only one P-38 attack the lead bomber - and it was from the rear. No. 323 caught fire and lost altitude, plowing down into the jungle below. There were no survivors. There can be no doubt that Barber was the pilot who shot down Admiral Yamamoto. For the most detailed analysis of this historic combat, the reader is advised to study **Attack on Yamamoto** by Carroll V. Glines, 1990, Orion Books, New York. Gline's definitive study should finally put the Lanphier myth to rest. Colonel Barber now resides in Oregon while Tom Lanphier, 71, passed away in San Diego, California on Thanksgiving Day, 1987.

The escort pilots made a number of claims when they returned to base. Tsujinoue - one plus another indefinite; Sugita - two; Hidaka - one indefinite; and Yanagiya - one indefinite. However, the only P-38 lost was that flown by Lieutenant Raymond K. Hine. He was certainly hit by Shoichi Sugita and may have fallen to him or to Kenji Yanagiya. Besby Holmes, hit by Tsujinoue in his fuel tank, made it safely home but not before stopping to refuel in the Russell Islands. None of the escort Zeros

The day after: Surviving members of the Yamamoto Mission pose for this group photo. They are, kneeling left to right: William E. Smith, Doug Canning, Besby Holmes, Rex Barber, John Mitchell, Louis Kittel and Gordon Whittaker. Standing, left to right: Roger Ames, Lawrence Graebner, Tom Lanphier, Delton Goerke, Julius Jacobson, Eldon Stratton, Albert Long, and Everett Anglin. (Rex T. Barber)

were lost and five of the six did not suffer damage. The sixth plane's condition is not known.

On the American side, the P-38s claimed three Zeros. Lanphier was given credit for one Zero; Barber and Holmes received credit for one Zero each and they shot the second Betty into the sea from which three survived. There is the possibility that Zeros from nearby Kahili Air Field took off and engaged the P-38s but further details are unknown.

The failure of the six Zero pilots to protect their commander-in-chief destroyed their morale and self dignity. The only way to redeem themselves was to die in combat to atone for their failure. In this regard, they were afforded every opportunity to do so. Within three months, four of the escort pilots were dead.

Zero 21s preparing for takeoff from Rabaul Airfield, 1943. (Maru)

The first to die was Chief Petty Officer Yoshimi Hidaka. He was shot down and killed on June 7, 1943 over the Russells. Lieutenant (jg) Takeshi Morizaki fell on June 16th over Lunga Point. Petty Officer First Class Toyomitsu Tsujinoue died on July 1st over Rendova, followed by Petty Officer Second Class Yasuji Okazaki on July 12th. Only one of the six would survive the war - Kenji Yanagiya. He was wounded in action on the June 7th mission to Guadalcanal, lost his right arm, and was sent back to Japan for hospitalization. He served out the remainder of the war as an instructor. Yanagiya now resides in Tokyo where he is in the real estate business.

Shoichi Sugita's luck continued to hold. He was full of remorse and hoped to die a glorious death, but he only got better. He threw all caution to the wind and hurled himself at the enemy. His extreme aggressiveness helped him survive overwhelming odds and added considerably to his victory total.

On August 16, 1943 Sugita's plane was hit in combat with F4U Corsairs near Ballale. He parachuted with burns and was returned to Japan for treatment.

By March 1944 Sugita was back in combat serving with the 263rd Kokutai from Truk to the Marianas. On July 8th, six Zeros under the command of Lieutenant Yasuhiro Shigematsu, the air group leader, were attacked by VF-31 Hellcats near Yap while enroute to the Palau Islands. In wild dogfighting Sugita was the only one to survive. He was transferred to the 201st Kokutai after this slaughter and saw further action in the Philippines. By the time he was reassigned to Japan in January 1945 he had claimed over 120 aerial victories.

Captain Minoru Genda was the mastermind behind the Pearl Harbor attack and led Japan's "Squadron of Experts" toward the end of the war.

Captain Minoru Genda, the master strategist, believed in turning back the American advance through air dominance. He was given an opportunity to prove his novel theory by organizing a special unit at Matsuyama Airfield on Shikoku Island, Japan. The 343 Kokutai was formed in December 1944 and was equipped with the latest fighter - the Shiden-Kai (George). Sugita was one of the pilots personally selected by Genda to fight with the new group. He was assigned to the 301 Squadron, headed by veteran pilot, Lieutenant Naoshi Kanno.

When American carrier groups launched a strike against Kure Harbor on March 19, 1945 Sugita and his wingmen fought superbly and claimed the destruction of three Hellcats. Because of his outstanding service record and the need to raise morale, he received a rare official (verbal) commendation from Admiral Soemu Toyoda the same month.

By this time, the war situation looked dismal for the Japanese as the Allies were tightening their noose around the Japanese homeland. Iwo Jima had fallen in February and Okinawa was about to be invaded. With its back against the wall, Japan began to send out wave after wave of Kamikazes (suicide planes) in a desperate attempt to halt the offensive. The Americans countered, attempting to neutralize the Kyushu-based airfields where many of the Kamikazes originated, and April 15, 1945 was another day of such air strikes.

One of the fighter pilots participating in the day's action was twenty-eight year old Lieutenant Commander Robert "Doc" Weatherup, executive officer of VF-46 on board the carrier **Independence**. A 1940 Naval Academy graduate, he had earned his pilot's wings in June 1943 and joined the newly commissioned VF-46 in April 1944. Air-to-air gunnery was his forte and he consistently had the best score in the Squadron. Weatherup attributed his shooting eye to previous training as an instructor and to his pheasant hunting days as a youth growing up on a dairy farm in upstate New York.

Fighter sweeps were launched at 1315 against three airfields on the southern tip of Kyushu, all in close proximity to each other. Units of Task Force 58.1 were to hit Kanoya, home base of the 343rd Kokutai. Task Force 58.2 targeted Kushira Airfield and Task Force 58.3 was assigned to assault Kanoya East. Each strike group had approximately thirty aircraft. Kanoya was designated as the secondary target for all groups if nothing worthwhile was found at the primaries.

Lieutenant Commander Weatherup led the Task Force 58.2 strike group, made up of eight VF-46 Hellcats and twenty more from **Randolph's** VF-12. The fighters launched approximately 300 miles from their targets.

The 301st Squadron of the 343rd Kokutai "Squadron of Experts" on Matsuyama Airfield, January 1945. Chief Petty Officer Shoichi Sugita is third from the right in the second row. Lieutenant Naoshi Kanno, squadron leader, is second from left, first row. Captain Minoru Genda is seated in the center.

Retired Commander Bob Weatherup recalls this mission:

"...I considered going in at high altitude (approximately 30,000 feet) as we had done during the many flights against the Tokyo area. However, I finally decided on about 15,000 feet even though 30,000 might have been 'safer' from an air-to-air point of view. I really hoped that we would achieve some degree of surprise and catch several aircraft on the ground. From that point of view, I didn't want to be too high when we started our attacks. That is, I wanted to be able to see what was going on at the airfields. On the other hand, I wanted some altitude for maneuver in case we were jumped by fighters from above. (The formation was really too big for a true low altitude approach.) Since we were over or near Japanese territory for a major part of our approach, I did not expect to get a complete surprise - especially insofar as anti-aircraft weapons were concerned. In summary, I picked a mid-altitude based on a variety of considerations, but I was really hoping to catch several aircraft on the ground."

The approach of enemy aircraft was detected and this information was passed along to the headquarters of the 343rd on Kanoya Airfield. Captain Genda ordered the eight Shiden-Kai Georges (301 Squadron) on standby, to scramble. Twenty-one year old Chief Petty Officer Shoichi Sugita was the first to spot the enemy planes as they ran to their mounts and he pointed them out to the other men.

Ensign Saburo Sakai, then attached as a training officer to the 701st Squadron, saw the futility of a takeoff. "Sugita, it's too late! Take cover!" he yelled, a warning that was ignored with fatal results.

As the Hellcats approached Kushira up Kagoshima Bay, Weatherup spotted activity on nearby Kanoya Airfield, his secondary target. He made a turn and announced to his flight: "I'm going to make my dive on the field nearest to us." He was followed by the other pilots of VF-46 while the VF-12 formation continued to the primary.

Ensign Saburo Sakai, one of Japan's most renowned aces, was a training officer in the 343 Kokutai. He urged Sugita to take cover as U.S. Navy fighters dove on their airfield, but his warning went unheeded.

Meanwhile Sugita jumped into his fighter, gunned the engine and taxied forward, followed by his wingman, Petty Officer Second Class Toyomi Miyazawa, the only aircraft of the unit to take off. When Weatherup's Hellcats had approached the field ground crews had bolted for cover, leaving the wheel blocks of the other Georges in place. Just as the other six pilots reached their aircraft, they were told to abort and none too soon. With the

The final moments of Chief Petty Officer Shoichi Sugita, April 15, 1945 over Kanoya Airfield. Lieutenant Commander Robert Weatherup delivers the fatal blows. (Depiction by Shori Tanaka.)

attackers already diving on them, they scattered for cover.

"As we approached Kanoya, I could see several aircraft taxiing and apparently preparing for takeoff," recalls Weatherup. "I decided to attack this airfield. I picked out an aircraft (or a decoy) in a revetment and fired my rockets at it and then strafed until I had to start my pull-out.

"As I was getting level again, I saw that two (or more) aircraft were starting their takeoff. I decided to take the lead aircraft, but was forced to pull pretty hard in a high tight turn of nearly 270 degrees to get on his tail. By this time, the lead aircraft was probably 400 feet and starting a slight turn. I decided to take the first aircraft, thinking that it was probably flown by a senior flight leader and that their formation might fall apart without the flight leader. I also presumed that some of my unit would take any following aircraft.

"With respect to the first aircraft, I was fortunate to have both altitude and speed advantage. I pulled a 'big lead' and waited until the wingspan of the target was thirty-five mils in my sight and started firing. At first I had a little too much lead and the target aircraft apparently saw my tracers and relaxed his turn. Almost immediately, I started to see 'flicks' where my bullets were hitting armor or heavy structure. Soon thereafter, the target aircraft started to nose over. I continued to fire until I had to pull up. The aircraft did not burn until it crashed although there may have been a little smoke."

Petty Officer Second Class Toyomi Miyazawa

Ensign Saburo Sakai, looking up from an air raid shelter below, was horrified to see Sugita's aircraft taking hits and going down. He never had a chance. Fully fueled and armed, the George exploded with a tremendous blast in a clearing near the airfield. "I didn't go over to the crash site," sighed Sakai. "What was the use? He was gone."

"As we turned toward our rendezvous," continued Weatherup, "I saw another Japanese fighter below me. I made an overhead run on him and also splashed this second aircraft."

Weatherup's second target was Petty Officer Second Class Toyomi Miyazawa. His George went down into the pine forest next to the airfield. He had managed to reach 400 feet when he was disabled.

Chief Petty Officer Shoichi Sugita received a posthumous double promotion to ensign. It was not Genda's policy to award such recognition to enlisted men. Sugita's special honor came from higher up. Today, more than forty-seven years after his death his family and old comrades come to Kanoya to pray at his crash site. There is also a small stone monument in the pine forest for Toyomi Miyazawa where he came to rest.

Robert Weatherup finished the war with those two victories. He retired from the Navy in 1961 after a distinguished career, then worked for McDonnell Aircraft until his retirement in 1982. He and his wife, Kay, have been active in church and community affairs. When asked what he would say to the mothers of the two pilots he had shot down, he replied, "Of course, I would simply say I was doing my job and presumably he was doing his job too." Bob Weatherup resides in San Jose, California.

"Doc" Weatherup, Executive Officer of VF-46.

Rex Barber, the pilot who downed Admiral Yamamoto (left), the author, and mission leader John W. Mitchell, in 1990

Retired Comdr. Bob Weatherup and Saburo Sakai meet for the first time at a Memorial Day reunion in 1982 in San Gabriel, CA.

The Yamamoto Mission living survivors in Fredericksburg, Texas, April 1988. Left to right: Roger Ames, Rex Barber, Doug Canning, Kenji Yanagiya, Delton Goerke, Julius Jacobson, Besby Holmes, John W. Mitchell, and Louis Kittel. (Yanagiya)

SOMEONE REMEMBERED

Second Lieutenant Wellman Howard Huey.

A telegram from the War Department always brought bad news. Mothers broke down and cried at their appearance. "It is with the deepest regret..." the telegram would start out. For the Huey family of Detroit, Michigan their telegram arrived to inform them that their son, Wellman, was missing in action on Valentine's Day 1943. He was a P-38 pilot with the 339th Fighter Squadron. It had only been ten and a half months since he had left home. At the time he was lost he had logged a total of 297 hours and fifteen minutes.

The 339th Fighter Squadron was activated on October 3, 1942. Initially equipped with the P-39 it was thrown into combat alongside the 67th Fighter Squadron based on Guadalcanal. As part of the 347th Fighter Group, the 339th scored its first victories on October 9, 1942 when Captain John W. Mitchell and First Lieutenants William S. Shaw and Fred V. Purnell each claimed a Japanese float plane.

Young Wellman Huey arrived on Guadalcanal as a volunteer replacement pilot on February 2, 1943. He had attended the University of Michigan briefly before transferring to the Detroit Institute of Technology. He had tried to enlist in the military even before the war but had been turned down for minor medical reasons. After Pearl Harbor, however, he had been accepted for flight training and won his wings and Second Lieutenant's commission at Luke Field in October 1942.

When he departed for the Pacific Huey brought along a U.S. flag that his uncle and namesake had carried into battle in World War I. The elder Wellman Huey, a Marine, had been killed in action in France and the flag had served as a sober memento to the family.

Second Lieutenant Wellman Huey kept a diary of his brief combat service in the Solomons and recorded thoughts of his first mission:

"Wednesday, 2/3/43: Went on my first mission today for high cover for some SBD's and TBF's. There were about twenty bombers, sixteen F4Fs, four P-40s and eight P-38s. Their mission was to bomb any shipping around Vella Lavella, but as there was none to be found, they bombed the Munda Air Field. No fighter opposition was met but they did throw up quite a bit of ack ack in our direction, which all fell below. We were bombed again tonight from high altitude but the bombs fell far off."

Huey's entry for February 10th, four days before his last mission, read: "Quite a day today. Took off with Rist on a search mission to Shortland. Couldn't see a thing though as the entire area was clouded over. On the way back as we came through a cloud, we ran upon a Mitsubishi Mark 01 Heavy Bomber. We jumped it at about 18,000 feet and when I last saw it, it was just a pool of burning oil and smoke on the surface of the water. Rist gets the credit for it as he had the left engine burning before I had made a pass but I still hit him with my share as I sat on his tail pumping lead from about 8,000 feet until just before he hit the water. It was only about five minutes from the time we first saw him until he hit the water, but everything was so clear and vivid that it seemed about an hour ago.

"Well, I have now tasted blood and am quite eager to get one for myself. We were mistaken about the cans (destroyers) that came down the other night; their purpose was to evacuate troops, not land them.

Guadalcanal is now entirely in our hands. I wonder where we will strike next."

On February 14, 1943 ten P-38s departed from their base at Henderson Field on Guadalcanal. They were joined by a dozen Corsairs from VMF-124 and some P-40s. Their mission was to escort nine PB4Ys (B-24s) on a strike against shipping in the Buin-Shortland Island area. The bombers succeeded in hitting several ships and inflicted damages to others. Trouble started when the combined force was coming off the bomb run.

Lieutenant Zenjiro Miyano was the air group commander of the 204th Kokutai. A superior fighter and leader, he had more than ten victories to his credit (sixteen victories at the time of death on June 16, 1943). Thirteen Zeros under Miyano's command scrambled into the air from Kahili Airfield within minutes of the raid followed by several float fighters. Among the other Zero pilots in action that day were Petty Officers Ryoji Ohara and Sei-Ichi Nakazawa.

Ohara was known among his peers as "The Killer of Rabaul". After completing flight training in July 1942 he had been shipped immediately to the battle front. He claimed most of his forty-eight victories in heavy fighting in the Solomons, New Guinea, and Rabaul. His classmate, Sei-Ichi Nakazawa, hailed from Nagano Prefecture, was born in 1920 and joined the Navy in 1940. He became a member of 204th Kokutai based at Buin and fought alongside Ohara.

In the wild melee that followed, First Lieutenant William M. Griffiths claimed a Zero and a probable. Captain James A. Geyer claimed two and a probable. First Lieutenant Brian W. Brown claimed a probable. Three Marine pilots each claimed a Zero. However, overall American losses were disastrous. Two B-24s, two F4Us, and four P-38s failed to return. The 339th lost four pilots: Lieutenants Joseph Finkenstein, Donald G. White, John R. Mulvey Jr. (rescued) and Wellman H. Huey.

The Japanese suffered only one aircraft loss, but claimed two B-24s, two F4Us, and four P-38s. Their claims were surprisingly accurate. Ohara and Nakazawa, along with others in their flight, pursued one bomber as far as Santa Isabel Island before shooting it down.

Major John W. Mitchell, Wellman Huey's commanding officer, had the arduous task of writing a letter to the Huey family. In a letter dated March 28, 1943, Major Mitchell wrote," Wellman was on an escort mission in a P-38 type airplane to Shortland Island at the southern end of Bougainville. When over the target, he and the rest of the flight were attacked by a greatly superior number of Japanese fighters. In the ensuing battle the flight became separated and no one saw Wellman go down, but he failed to ever show up again. There were several other islands within fifty miles or so but it is doubtful that he made any of these as he would have probably been found by now."

Major Mitchell ended his letter with, "Wellman was one of the best liked men in the squadron and I considered him to be one of my best young pilots...You and your family have my utmost sympathy in losing so fine a lad."

Warrant Officer Ryoji Ohara, Yokosuka Kokutai, 1944, in the home defense. (Ryoji Ohara)

The War Department declared that Second Lieutenant Wellman Howard Huey, 0732254, Air Corp, was presumed to have died on February 14, 1943 in aerial combat in the Shortlands. He was promoted to the rank of First Lieutenant on October 30 1945. The war ended, and except for the family of Wellman Huey, he was forgotten, just another statistic. But the War Department was wrong, and someone else remembered Wellman Huey.

In 1976, the 204th Kokutai Association published a book entitled **Rabaul**. It was a historical work concerning their old fighter group and included recollections from surviving members. On one of the pages, it described the combat of February 14, 1943. "On this day, our combat results were two B-24s, two F4Us, and four P-38s. One P-38 pilot parachuted down and was captured. This young twenty-two year old Second Lieutenant was a graduate of Michigan University." It went on to say that Petty Officer Sei-Ichi Nakazawa was very impressed with the young American's spirit, which he noted in his diary.

The information about Wellman Huey's capture went undiscovered in the United States until 1989. A check of several universities in Michigan revealed that Wellman Huey had attended the University of Michigan from September 1937 through May 1938. He was a student in the College of Literature, Science, and the Arts. He was indeed twenty-two years old at the time of his capture and his rank was second lieutenant. None of the other two missing pilots had lived in Michigan. In official records, he was declared missing in action and presumed dead. After forty-six years it was found that Wellman Huey had been taken prisoner.

On August 23, 1989 an article appeared in the **Detroit News** telling the story of the P-38 pilot and the search for his next of kin. The response was immediate. Mr. Don H. Huey, a retired forty-five year veteran of TRW, Michigan Division, answered. Wellman was his younger brother.

In a letter dated August 31, 1989, Mr. Huey wrote, "You can't imagine how surprised I was to read the article in the Detroit News about my younger brother Wellman. It brought back memories I hadn't thought of in years. My brother's disappearance and the notification we received from the Army Air Force always left us (my parents and sister and I) with an empty feeling of 'not knowing'. We could only conjecture as to what happened to him on his last flight with no real concrete evidence to validate it."

On December 16, 1991, Mr. Jiro Yoshida of Tokyo, a former Zero pilot and goodwill ambassador, made contact with Ryoji Ohara. When asked if he had ever met Wellman Huey, Ohara's response was affirmative. Someone had remembered. In a series of conversations, Ohara told this story:

Petty Officer Sei-Ichi Nakazawa in 1941 as a flight trainee at Tsuchiura Air Base. (Ryoji Ohara)

"After the dogfight on February 14, 1943 we were told by the commander that an enemy pilot had parachuted down over our airfield and was captured. Around dusk while going back to our barracks after the mission, we decided to go and rough up this guy. We saw him squatting down in front of the headquarters building. He was tied to a tree and there was a guard watching him. He was wearing his flight suit, boots, and flight helmet with goggles. The American was smiling and was polite and talkative, but we couldn't understand him. An interpreter told us that he wanted to present his flight helmet to us as a gift. We learned that he was a graduate of Michigan University, age twenty-two, that he went to flight school and became a fighter pilot in the P-38. He was a good looking fellow, intelligent, and had a fine attitude and he made a very good impression on us all. Nobody wanted to beat him up, give him a hard time.

"The American told the interpreter that his biggest concern was getting out of here. He wanted to be shipped out on the first available transport plane. Buin was at the very front lines and we did not have facilities for prisoners. In fact, he was our first American prisoner. It was really brave of him to have made that request. I heard later that he was sent to Rabaul, but I can't confirm if he was actually sent there or not. Anyway, I remember him as though it was only yesterday. He and I were both born in 1921 and we were the same age."

A detailed check of listings of all known prisoners of war kept at Rabaul failed to find any evidence of Wellman Huey. The Japanese Army's 17th Military Police Unit would have had jurisdiction over the prisoner. The unit's commander, Provost Lieutenant Colonel Tadao Egusa took all but ten of his men to oppose the U.S. Marines landing on Guadalcanal. They all perished. The remaining ten men left on Rabaul were under the command of a second lieutenant.

A new Army Kempei-Tai (military police) unit arrived on Rabaul March 22, 1943. It was headed by Provost Lieutenant Colonel Satoru Kikuchi, now deceased. The Rabaul Military Police Section (6th Field Kempei-Tai) had about fifty men. Inquiries with two surviving members of this unit concerning Wellman Huey proved negative. They did not recall him.

It is certain that Wellman Huey was not imprisoned in Rabaul for very long. It is possible that he was shipped out to Japan for further interrogation and lost en route. However, a more like scenario was that he was never turned over to the Army Kempei-Tai. Wellman Huey may have been executed. The Japanese Navy did not operate POW facilities on Rabaul. They did not, as a rule, keep prisoners on Rabaul. If such was the case, Huey was probably buried in an unmarked grave.

Warrant Officer Ryoji Ohara ended the war as a member of the Yokosuka Kokutai. He joined the postwar Maritime Self-Defense Force and retired as a lieutenant commander in 1970 later establishing an airline pilot's training school near Haneda Airport before retiring in 1990.

Petty Officer Sei-Ichi Nakazawa, who was so impressed with Wellman Huey that he noted their meeting in his personal diary, was killed in action over Buin on July 18, 1943. Ohara now has possession of his friend's diary.

Don H. Huey wrote a letter to Ryoji Ohara on March 4, 1992:

"It was so hard on my family receiving the news my brother was 'missing in action'. Out of the five members of my family, I am the only living person. Once I find out what happened to Wellman, I will finally be able to put him to rest in my mind. You have helped me get closer to that objective. I appreciate your input. World War II was devastating to both of our countries. My heart goes out to those who lost loved ones on both sides of the ocean."

Forty-six years is a long time to wait for a partial solution. Don Huey's search for the final answer continues.

Ryoji Ohara as he appears today. (Ryoji Ohara)

Wellman Huey as a young flight trainee in 1942 at Cal-Aero Flight Academy in Ontario, California.

NIGHT FIGHTER OVER GUADALCANAL

Second Lieutenant Henry Meigs II and his comrades were irritated. They didn't mind putting in a hard day's work fighting the enemy, but robbing them of their sleep was downright despicable.

The Japanese routinely sent night hecklers down to Guadalcanal. These aircraft were known as "Washing Machine Charlie" because of the dissonant engine noise produced by their unsynchronized propellers. The Americans retaliated in kind; in addition to bombs, they also pelted their counterparts with empty beer and Coke bottles.

Captain Takashi Miyazaki, commander of the 4th Air Group at Rabaul stated in his postwar interrogation: "At first we sent one or two planes down at night if the weather was favorable just to keep the forces there disturbed. Both landplanes and seaplanes were used."

However, since anti-aircraft fire never hit anything, the night missions continued. Although Japanese bombing did very little damage, it did fray a lot of nerves and the din of anti-aircraft fire was an added irritant.

"It was widely discussed among our fighter pilots that it should be easy work for any of us to end this annoyance by use of our aircraft (P-38s) aided by large searchlights all over the island," recalls Meigs. "The risk of flying through or over our own anti-aircraft fire seemed to us minimal, in view of their poor success rate."

This radical idea had merit. The twenty-two year old New Yorker who arrived in the South Pacific with the 339th Fighter Squadron, was certain that the P-38 Lightning could alleviate his comrades' collective insomnia.

Lt. Henry Meigs II of the 339th Ftr. Sq. and the 6th Night Ftr. Sq. (Credit: American Fighter Aces Assn.)

A Mitsubishi G4M "Betty", the standard day and night medium bomber of the Japanese Navy as depicted by Shori Tanaka.

In mid-1943 a squadron of P-70s had arrived on Guadalcanal for night fighting duty. Developed by Douglas, these twin engined, low level, radar equipped variants were interim nightfighters until the Northrup P-61 "Black Widow" became available. It had a maximum level speed of 329 mph and a theoretical maximum service ceiling of 28,250 feet. But when sent aloft to take care of Washing Machine Charlie, the low level P-70 generally could not reach sufficient altitude to intercept.

Henry Meigs and several other day fighter pilots of the 347th Fighter Group were detached to the 6th Night Fighter Squadron. At 0110 hours on August 15, 1943 Meigs scored his first night victory (and proved his point) by downing a Betty bomber southwest of Fighter Two Airfield. He recalls, "...it proved to be just as simple a task as it had appeared from the ground. As soon as the radar-directed searchlight picked out the target, the rest of the lights focused on it and it became as clearly illuminated as a star in the night sky."

On the night of September 20/21, 1943 six Mitsubishi G4M Betty bombers of the 702nd Kokutai took off from their base at Rabaul, New Britain Island. Their mission was to bomb the Fighter Two Airfield on Guadalcanal. Leading this night assault was Lieutenant Tadasu Itakura (pilot). His crew consisted of Petty Officers First Class Shigenobu Matsuoka (co-pilot), Sen Osawa (mechanic), Warrant Officer Takayuki Isezaki (observer), Petty Oficers Third Class Takeyoshi Nagano and Tsuyoshige Oki, Naval Pilot First Class Kinji Sueoka, Petty Officer Second Class Isao Komatsu (radioman),

The unsuspecting Japanese had no idea that they were being set up. Meigs remembers, "...I was scrambled upon ground radar reports of two bogies at a certain altitude and course - about 25,000 feet - and a southerly heading. By the time I reached altitude and turned inland the search lights were on the first Betty and all our ninety millimeter guns were filling the sky with brilliant flashes, but nowhere close to the enemy - nor to me, fortunately.

"As I closed on this Betty I tried to fly directly astern but keeping back far enough to stay out of the search light aura. At about 200 feet I fired the four .50 caliber machine guns at the right wing-root. Before I could squeeze the trigger on the 20mm cannon the Betty burst into flame and nosed over in a steep dive toward the ground.

An early scoreboard for the 6th NF Sq. naming pilots of both P-70 and P-38 aircraft.

The communications shack of the 6th NF Sq. helped vector pilots aloft to approaching Japanese bombers.

"Enemy night fighter!" screamed a radioman into his R/T. The bombers took evasive action. The second plane of the second element was caught in the searchlight pattern.

"As I had been advised from the ground there was another bomber close by, I held altitude and turned in the direction of the search light pattern," remembers Meigs. "The big light, known as 'Eveready Senior', immediately picked out a second Betty at some distance behind me. Turning almost 180 degrees I poured on throttle to close the gap before the enemy had run out of the lights. In so doing I closed too fast and had to cut throttle and bank steeply to keep from overrunning the target. After killing some speed I again approached the tail of this aircraft but came up so close I was in the lights myself. The tail-gunner must have seen me for I could see his gun flashes and felt my ship take a pretty good hit from machine gun fire. Again aiming at the right wing-root I pulled both triggers (.50 caliber and 20mm.) and exploded the target instantly. Radar on the ground reported all clear and I dropped down for a landing."

This was Henry Meigs' third night victory. The crew of this second Betty consisted of Petty Officers First Class Masao Kisuberi (pilot) and Hiroshi Unzai (observer), Petty Officers Second Class Yasuji Kukizono (radioman) and Yoshio Ishida (mechanic), and Petty Officers Third Class Yasumasa Yamada, Tsumio Kaneo, Katsutoshi Umeda, Shigeo Osaka, and Shigeo Mikami.

Meigs continues, "After parking my aircraft I was told both Bettys were aflame in the air before the first one hit the ground, and that the whole thing had taken only about sixty seconds. My crew chief also showed me a hole in my horizontal stabilizer big enough to put my head through - which I did, and had my picture taken that way. Whatever became of that picture I'm sorry to say I don't know.

"I don't think the family of any of these aircrews would be very happy to hear such news, but those men were, as we were, trained to do the jobs they'd undertaken on behalf of their country and unfortunately, some had to die in the process. I'm happy to have survived and glad to see relations between the Japanese people and the American people have been cordial over the past forty-three years."

Lieutenant Tadasu Itakura's pocket diary was found in the wreckage of his aircraft on Guadalcanal. It was translated by Third Marine Division Intelligence. A copy of this diary lay undisturbed in the Australian Archives until 1989. An effort will be undertaken to notify the next of kin of the bomber crewmen surrounding the circumstances of their deaths.

Henry Meigs soon returned to the 339th Fighter Squadron, 347th Group and ended the war with six victories, the Silver Star, DFC, Air Medal and clusters. He served for twenty-three years as a circuit judge in Kentucky and now practices law in Louisville.

The Detachment B, 6th Night Fighter Squadron, scored a total of nine victories during their tour of the Solomon Islands, a third of them by Henry Meigs. The first two kills were made by P-70 crews, the other seven by 6th pilots who had converted to the P-38 and by detached day fighter pilots like Meigs.

Lt. Henry Meigs receives the Silver Star for his night flying heroics at an award ceremony on Guadalcanal. In the front row receiving awards Meigs is second from the left. On his right is Lt. Col. Aaron Tyer, CO, 18th Ftr. Grp., At the far left is Maj. Gen. Nathan Twining, Commanding Thirteenth Air Force. (Henry Meigs II)

AMBUSH OVER AMOY HARBOR

"I was shot down only once, but never considered myself defeated in the air," recalled former Japanese Navy Warrant Officer Takeo Tanimizu. His first encounter with P-51 Mustangs had nearly cost him his life and would haunt him for years afterwards.

It was November 3, 1944. Tanimizu and his wingman, Leading Flight Seaman Manabu Ito both of the Tainan Kokutai, had been providing air cover for a convoy of ships entering Amoy Harbor, China. It was a cloudy and dismal morning and their mission had been uneventful. After two hours it was time to land. Tanimizu lowered his landing gear and slid back the canopy with Ito trailing close behind. They were just entering their landing pattern.

First Lieutenant John W. Bolyard and Captain Paul J. Reis of the 74th Fighter Squadron were, at the moment, approaching Amoy Harbor. The two P-51s had taken off from Kanchow at 1315 hours, looking for enemy shipping and ground activity in the Foochow area. They were following the coastline up to Amoy.

"Zekes!" shouted Bolyard over the radio. He had spotted Tanimizu and Ito in their landing approach and selected Ito while Reis went after Tanimizu.

"I was going through my landing procedures when all of a sudden, my wing was punctured by bullets," recalled Tanimizu. "I looked back and didn't see anything unusual, so I assumed that my wingman had fumbled with the throttle and accidentally squeezed off a short burst." (The machine gun firing lever was connected to the throttle.) Ito was an inexperienced pilot with less than 150 flight hours."

However, it was Captain Reis, firing from extreme range, who scored hits on Tanimizu's wingtip. Lieutenant Bolyard closed in on Ito, who spotted the Mustangs and made a sharp left turn at 1,200 feet, albeit too late. Bolyard came in from slightly underneath and behind, firing a short burst from 500 yards that promptly registered. Ito's Zero exploded in midair and fell into the harbor. Bolyard dived down to fifty feet, then zoomed up to catch Tanimizu in his gunsight.

"I was unaware of what was happening behind me until I got another hit in the wing," said Tanimizu. "Damn, that idiot," he cursed thinking that Ito had squeezed off another accidental burst. He looked back and was horrified to see his wingman going down in a ball of fire.

Tanimizu was jolted into action. He opened full throttle, raised his flaps, and tried to retract his undercarriage. The landing gear seemed to take forever. Could his hydraulics have been hit? Tanimizu tried to zigzag his way out of the line of fire, but Bolyard had him boresighted. Suddenly, puncture holes walked up the wing and exploded the wing fuel tank. Flaming gasoline spewed into the open cockpit.

Warrant Officer Takeo Tanimizu, Taiwan 1944.

Leading Flight Seaman Manabu Ito, standing center.

"I didn't have my gloves on and the flames were burning my face, neck, and arms. I was thrashing about wildly, trying to extinguish the fire on me," said Tanimizu. "At the same time, my plane was out of control, going almost straight up. And then I thought - so this is where I'm going to die."

First Lieutenant John W. Bolyard.

Captain Paul J. Reis and his P-51B.

In the life and death struggle, the instinct for self-preservation took hold. Seconds seemed like forever as Tanimizu quickly assessed his predicament. "I'm badly burned, but I haven't been hit by bullets. I may still have a chance. I've got to get out now."

The Zero was prone to explode after taking a few hits and Tanimizu knew this too well. His burning crate was a time bomb. He started to climb out when his foot caught in the canopy. He was slammed back against the fuselage and the Zero continued its vertical climb on fire. The situation looked hopeless. Then, he found himself falling away.

Bolyard saw Tanimizu going down. He noted in his mission report, "Plane flamed and pilot climbed out and bailed at 250 feet. Chute and plane flamed and pilot and plane fell into the harbor. Chute believed to have opened just before pilot hit the bay."

Tanimizu's parachute popped open and the tremendous jerk stunned him. He became entangled in the shroud lines, going down head first. Struggling to right himself, he managed to assume a horizontal position before being slammed violently into the sea. A high surface wind blew the silk away and he quickly released his harness. Salt water on his blistering wounds was torturous, and he was forced to tread water in high surf for a couple of hours until rescued by two Chinese off the beach.

Anti-aircraft guns began to open up on the pair of Mustangs, so they quickly left the area. Lieutenant Bolyard, who received credit for the destruction of the two Zeros, became an Ace on December 27,1944 when he shot down his fifth enemy aircraft. He survived the war and lives in Florida. Captain Paul J. Reis was lost in action on December 8, 1944 in aerial combat near Nanking.

The Japanese Navy notified the parents of Manabu Ito that their son had died a heroic death in a big dogfight. Tanimizu had the grim task of writing them a letter and told them the true circumstances of his death. He enclosed a small traditional sum of money, but never heard back from them. "Perhaps they were angry with me that I lost their son," he sighed.

Tanimizu's first encounter with the Mustangs was nearly terminal. He spent over a month in a Taiwan hospital and was not fully recovered when he volunteered for the Kamikaze suicide operations. Although initially rejected he tried again, when an admiral scolded him. "Nonsense," said the the admiral sharply. "You're not in any condition to fly. You will go back to Japan and recover first." Tanimizu returned to the homeland and was assigned to the 203rd Kokutai as an instructor.

Takeo Tanimizu survived the war with thirty-two victories and now resides in Osaka. When asked if he would be interested in meeting John Bolyard, the Mustang Ace who shot him down, he replied with a chuckle, "Gee, what would I say to him?"

Takeo Tanimizu as he appears today. Mt. Fuji in background.

THE LORD'S PRAYER
By
Minoru Fujita and Henry Sakaida

Every war has its "Unknown Soldier". We pay homage to our own at the Tomb of the Unknown Soldier at Arlington, across from Washington, D.C. But for Minoru Fujita, a former gunboat commander of the Japanese Navy's 8th Submarine Base Unit, his Unknown Soldier was in his heart and mind. The soldier had been his enemy. This is Fujita's story.

Rabaul, January 15, 1945. "The enemy soldier brought before me is as still as a log, his eyes closed. The dark green uniform has absorbed sea water and is clinging tight to his body. His face is deadly pale, his lips parched and colorless. His hair is brown and crewcut, his forehead is broad, his ears large. He is slim of build and looks not much different from me in height and weight. He is the first Caucasian enemy I have encountered in the Pacific War.

"Looking more closely, I notice that the upper part of his left uniform sleeve is tattered and the flesh is torn; deep within, I can see something white. The bleeding has stopped, but it is a serious wound. I order one of my men to bring a blanket to cover him.

"It is sunset and a light evening breeze has come up. Lieutenant Miyajima, the medical officer who landed by submarine a few weeks ago, has begun treating the wound. Has the wound become numb, I wonder - there is no sign of pain. My eyes are riveted on the white bandage going round and round his upper left arm. It is the first pure white bandage I have seen on Rabaul; perhaps Miyajima brought it from Japan.

"After treating the wound, the Doctor reported to headquarters by field telephone on the condition of the prisoner. He returned and relayed to me the orders of the commander: "I am sending an investigating officer, so you must not let him die. Take all necessary measures to ensure his survival until then."

"There is a little color coming back to his cheek now, perhaps out of relief for having his wound treated. He opens his eyes slightly and asks for water. I say "No," because with such a serious wound, water would kill him. Lieutenant Miyajima, standing by me, agrees that giving him water or letting him sleep would mean death. He must be kept alive at all cost.

"In a loud voice, I start to question him. I am the only one who speaks a little English. I ask his name and he replies, 'Keefer.'

"Keefer? Why, I know this name! It is a name indelibly associated with a memory of my youth.

"During the 1932 Olympic competition held in Los Angeles, Japanese swimmers such as Kiyokawa (now a member of the International Olympic Committee) and Iriye

Minoru Shinohara (later Fujita) as an Ensign, Japanese Navy.

were fully expected to take the top three medals in the 200 meter backstroke competition, based on their performances in the earlier elimination races. To those Japanese who firmly believed that the Rising Sun flag and the "Kimigayo" (Japanese National Anthem) would dominate the Olympic Stadium that day, it had been a shock and bitter disappointment that a little-talked about American swimmer had snatched away the victory. His name had been Adolf Keefer, the same, I thought, as this prisoner's.

"His rank is lieutenant, his age two years younger than mine. The speed with which airmen are promoted is the same in the Japanese military, I say to myself. He replies smoothly to my questions regarding his family, education, base from which he launched, the number and types of fighters and bombers based there, etc. Perhaps he feels relieved that there is someone who can understand English He seems to be gradually regaining his strength.

"Yet, I marvel. With his wounded arm, he had been swimming in the sea snake and shark infested Bay of Rabaul for several hours, and had tried numerous times to escape out to the open sea. I want to salute this courageous enemy. I feel no hatred for his attacks on us just a few hours ago.

"A twin-engined flying boat, protected by two fighter escorts, had flown in from the mouth of the bay and twice tried to land and pick him up. Each time, however,

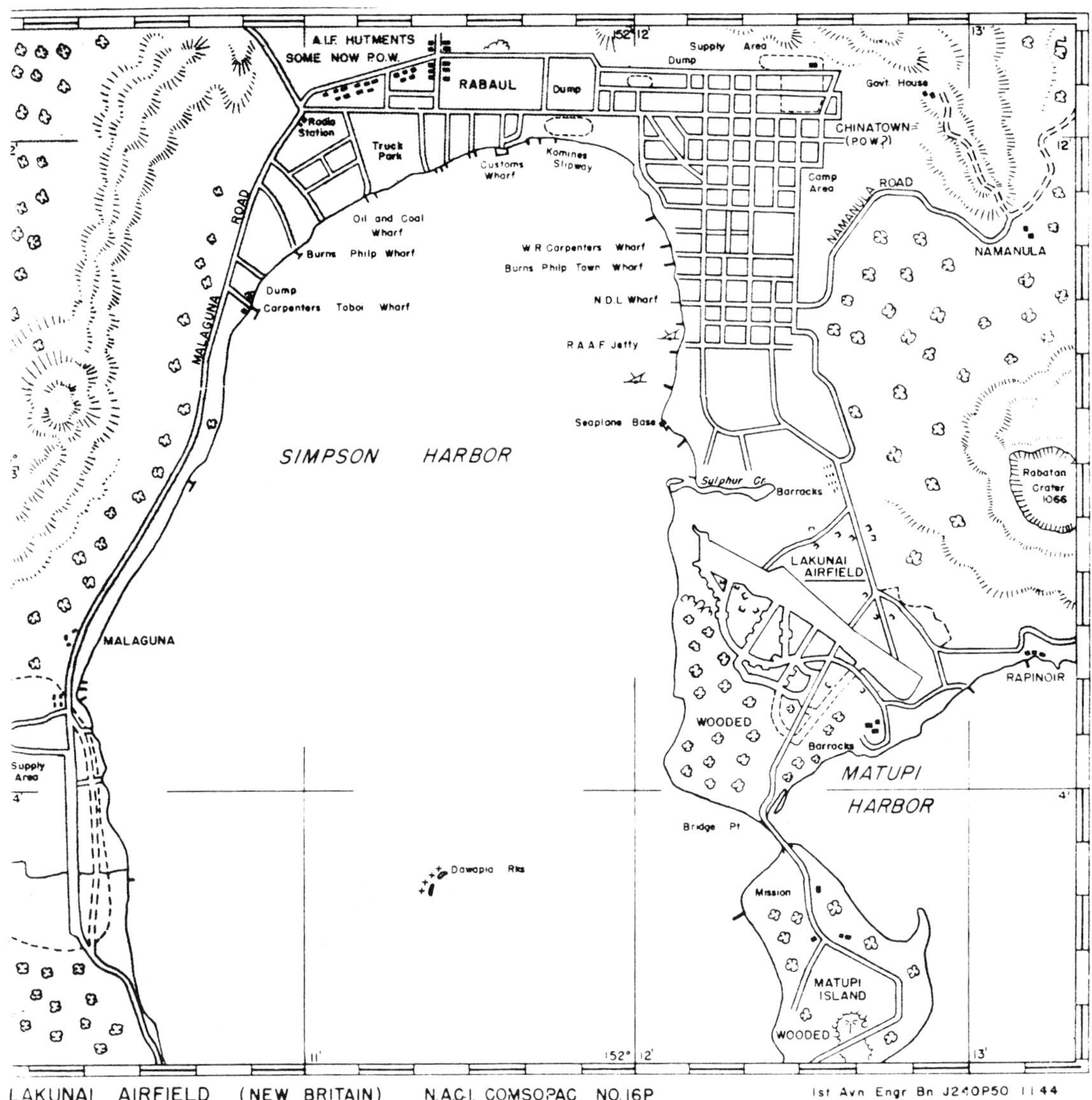

Simpson Harbor, Rabaul. Keefe swam ashore on Dawapia Rocks (known as Beehives) where he was eventually picked up by the Japanese.

they were repelled by machine gun fire from the Japanese position around Matupit (Matsushima), and had to give up. After they had flown away, he swam to Center Rock and collapsed on the beach. It was there that he was picked up by one of our small landing boats. I imagined how he must have felt being stranded in the midst of hostile forces, wounded, and having to watch his would-be rescuers flying away. I felt sorry for him.

"Suddenly, he looked intently at me and asked me to 'play'. What can he mean, 'play' in his wounded state? Then I realized that he meant 'pray'. But I know no English words of prayer. Has he imagined me to be a chaplain? He repeats, 'Pray for me.' I recall The Lord's Prayer.

"There used to be a Christian church in the neighborhood where I grew up. When I was still in school, a minister named Reverend Yokomizu, who had just returned from America, was assigned there. He and his wife started an English class at night for young people, so a classmate and I signed up. The very first thing we were taught there, and made to memorize, was The Lord's Prayer. After that came The Star Spangled Banner, Row, Row, Row Your Boat, and others. All were used to correct our English pronunciation. It would appear that the things imprinted on the mind of a sixteen or seventeen year old are never forgotten. It is already on the tip of my tongue: 'Our Father Who art in heaven...'

"When I say, 'Let's pray the Lord's Prayer,' his face tenses momentarily and he sighed deeply. Seeing this reaction, I hesitate, wondering if this was meant to be a prayer for a dying person. But his lips are already moving, mumbling the words of the prayer. In a loud voice, I join in, 'Thy kingdom come, Thy will be done on earth...'

"I fix my eyes on his and pray he does not die. He looks up at me and prays to God for salvation. Our eyes are linked in a single gaze, the words of the prayer voiced in unison. Enemy, ally, there is no longer any distinction. We are just two human beings, joining our hearts in prayer.

"For Thine is the kingdom, and the power, and the glory...Amen.' We finish, and he seems relieved; he says 'Thank you' and closes his eyes. There is something glinting in the corner of his eye.

"Will this gravely wounded prisoner be able to survive on this island with hardly any medical supplies and nothing to eat but sweet potatoes for nourishment? Even for us, it's only two or three potatoes and grass in a salt soup twice a day. If we get sick or injured, there isn't any medicine to speak of. The last dose of malaria medicine we had was one year ago. But somehow, we're still alive. 'Don't give up, Keefer. Don't die!' I found myself shouting in my heart.

"After a while, a truck pulls up and an officer gets out with four or five men. The officer writes down the things I learned form the prisoner, then questions the medical officer about the condition of his injury. When he is finished he directs his men to carry Keefer onto the truck.

"It is getting quite dark already. Keefer has raised his head slightly from the stretcher and is waving his right hand at me. In the dusk, his palm becomes a patch of white that burns deep into my vision, to remain for a long, long time."

The "Unknown Soldier" who touched Minoru Fujita's heart haunted him for the next forty-two years. Just who was this "Keefer" and was that really his name? Or had the young lieutenant misunderstood or even imagined it? It wasn't until 1987 that he would finally fill that void in his life.

The search for "Keefer" began in 1983. "Rabaul didn't have seasons, so it was hard to say when this incident occurred," lamented Fujita. "I believe it was either in late 1943 or early 1944. I'm not certain about his nationality either, but thought he could have been Australian." Intensive research eliminated the possibility that he could have been an American or an Australian. The search was complicated because all the records for 1943 and 1944 proved negative. As it turned out, Fujita was over a year off. The incident had occurred on January 15, 1945.

In 1987, the mystery of "Keefer" was solved when Australian aviation historian Lex McAulay located a document containing the names of civilians and Allied prisoners kept on Rabaul by the Japanese Navy. And there was the name: "Frank George Keefe - New Zealander, P.O.W. 1/15/45, Flight Lieut." The RNZAF mission report for this day confirmed the rescue attempt as seen through the eyes of Fujita. When shown a small photo copy of Keefe, Fujita studied it intensely for several moments and finally exclaimed, "Yes, yes, this was Keefe!"

Francis (Frank) George Keefe was born in Auckland, New Zealand in 1916. He was actually an O'Keefe, but dropped the "O" due to anti-Irish feelings. Frank graduated from Sacred Heart College and was employed as a driver mechanic while waiting to be accepted into the Royal New Zealand Air Force (RNZAF). Accepted for flight training as an airman pilot in December 1941, he was awarded his flying badge and commissioned as a pilot officer in September 1942. After serving as an instructor in various units and undergoing training in the new F4U Corsair, he departed for the front in October 1944.

The Japanese stronghold at Rabaul, New Britain had been ravaged by bombing and bypassed by Allied Forces in their drive north; however, it hadn't been entirely

F/L F.G. KEEFE
Auckland
14 SQUADRON

Flt. Sgt. Bryan Cox of 16 Squadron RNZAF. January 15, 1945, the date of the fateful mission to Rabaul was his twentieth birthday. His trusty Corsair #5261 brought him safely home. (Bryan Cox)

RNZAF Corsairs enroute from Guadalcanal to their new base on Green Island, 115 miles east of Rabaul. (Bryan Cox)

neutralized. Constant air raids chipped away at Japanese resistance.

January 15, 1945 marked one of the blackest days in RNZAF history. Orders were given to 14,16, and 24 Squadrons to reconnoiter enemy airfields at Rabaul and to attack targets of opportunity. The Kiwis were warned not to fly any lower than 10,000 feet while over the harbor and airfields these areas being ringed with highly accurate anti-aircraft batteries.

Thirty-six Corsairs took off from their base on Green Island and Bougainville in the predawn darkness. Advance flights from Green arrived early over Rabaul and proceeded to fly routine reconnaissance for about an hour and a half. The tranquility was broken at 0900 when the bombardment of Toboi Wharf, on the edge of Rabaul Township, began. Anti-aircraft response was tremendous. The lead Corsair planted its bomb squarely on target and each aircraft followed in a diving attack at very short intervals. Fifteen minutes into the attack, tragedy struck.

Flight Lieutenant Frank Keefe of 14 Squadron dove down from 15,000 feet. A direct hit from a 70mm gun shattered his right wing at 8,000 feet altitude. Flight Sergeant Norm Rosser of 24 Squadron had just pulled out of a dive when he caught sight of Keefe's flaming aircraft (NZ 5413) flashing past only a few yards away. The pilot bailed out at 2,000 feet, an inviting target for all the shore gunners. The hapless aviator floated down into the middle of Simpson Harbor in a hail of machine gun and small arms fire.

As soon as Keefe hit the water, the mission changed. Air cover was commenced immediately with daring, low-level strafing attacks along the shore to protect their downed comrade. Inflating his Mae West, he discarded his dinghy. He had to remain low in the water to present a smaller target. Keefe was a very strong swimmer and broke for the harbor entrance.

An American Catalina flying boat arrived later and began circling the harbor, its pilot coolly requesting

A New Zealand PV-1 Ventura was used to drop two native rafts to Keefe in Simpson Harbor (Bryan Cox)

permission to land and pick up the downed pilot. Permission was denied as a successful rescue was deemed impossible. But the Dumbo pilot was reluctant to abandon the downed flyer and, escorted by a pair of fighters, the bold Yank made two attempts to land. Heavy machine gun fire finally convinced him that rescue was beyond hope.

Frank Keefe was determined to swim out of the harbor, but he was being swept back by strong tides. Personnel back at base jammed into the radio room, listening in on the radio conversations over Rabaul between the pilots. Everyone was hanging on by their fingernails as the intense drama continued. It was now reported that Keefe was no longer making any progress.

Flight Sergeant Bryan Cox recalls the frenzied activity that followed, "While sections of Corsairs kept watch overhead to prevent attempts by the Japanese to capture the swimmer, who was wearing his Mae West, plans were made at Green Island to get natives to construct two bamboo rafts that would float low in the water and be dropped from a Ventura just prior to dusk."

The finished rafts were quickly loaded into the bomb bay. There was no problem in getting a dozen volunteers to escort the bomber to Rabaul. The fighters were to bomb and strafe the shore while the Ventura dropped the rafts to Keefe. At 1730, the rescue group was airborne. Squadron Leader Paul Green, commanding officer of 16 Squadron, led the mission.

When the group arrived over the harbor, Keefe had been treading water for over nine hours. The Kiwis went to work, chewing up the coastal gun batteries in a diversionary attack while the Ventura streaked in low. Squadron Leader Green flew in front of the bomber and fired his guns in the water to show the target; Flight Sergeant Cox followed the bomber and fired his guns to signal the drop. The rafts were released and landed close to Keefe, but he made no effort to retrieve them. He appeared motionless, draped over a small log.

There was nothing more that could be done now. Reluctantly, each pilot bade farewell to their downed comrade and started the long journey home, not realizing that a violent storm front had crossed their return route. The Corsair pilots became disoriented in bad weather and seven brave men lost their lives.

Keefe managed to struggle ashore on a small outcropping of rocks in the middle of the harbor. Lieutenant Minoru Shinohara (he changed his name to Fujita after the war), had been directing his men in gardening when a spotter notified him of a swimmer in the water. He could see Keefe clearly from shore. After the enemy aircraft departed, he ordered three of his men to take a Daihatsu landing craft and retrieve the downed flyer. Keefe was brought ashore, then carried on a stretcher inland where he was questioned by Shinohara. Although he was free with his answers, it was later learned that he gave false information. The gravely wounded prisoner was transferred by his captors to Naga Naga, imprisoned in a cave and died on January 30, 1945 due to blood poisoning and lack of medical treatment. Keefe was married at the time but had no children and was 28 years old, the same as Shinohara.

Minoru Fujita was deeply saddened to learn in 1987 that Keefe had died of his wounds. A compassionate man, Fujita had expressed hope that the prisoner had survived. "I would like to tell his next of kin what a brave

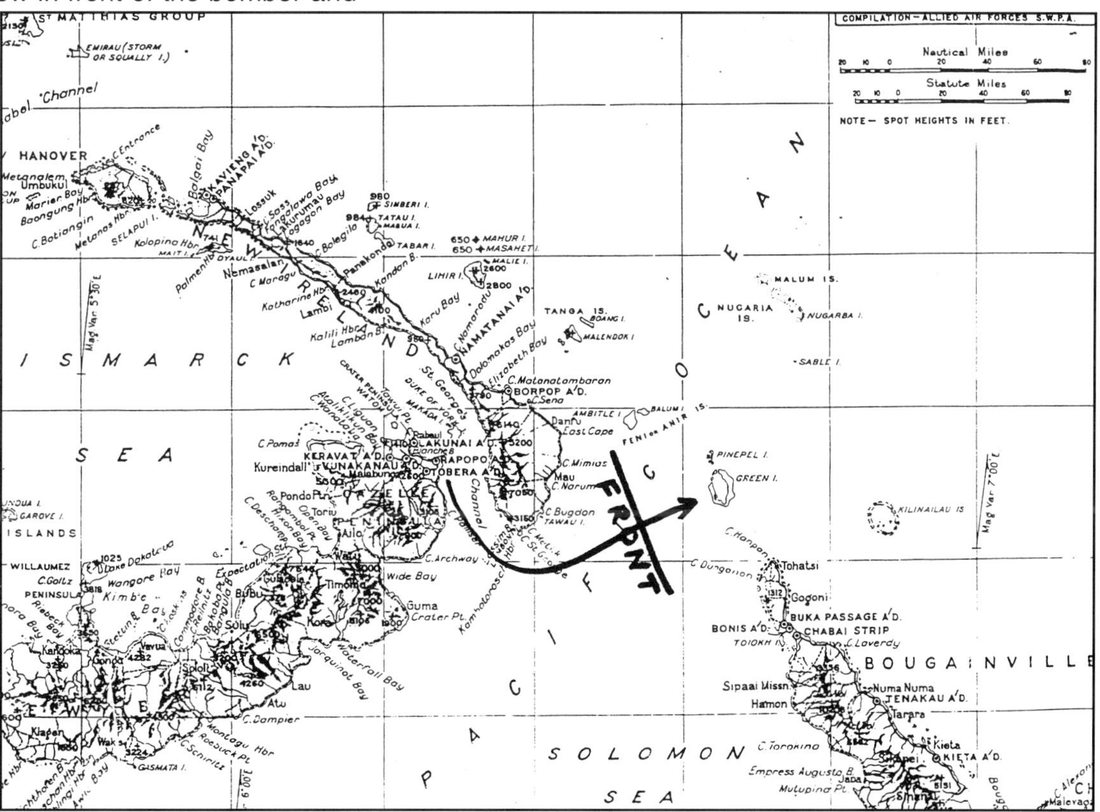

Returning Kiwis ran into a violent storm on their way back to Green Island. Bryan Cox shows the storm front. (Courtesy Bryan Cox)

F/L B.S. HAY
Taihape
14 SQUADRON

F/O A.N. SAWARD
Pukekohe
14 SQUADRON

F/SGT I.J. MUNRO
Wellsford
14 SQUADRON

These seven RNZAF pilots were lost in a severe weather front on January 15, 1945 returning from the attempt to save Frank Keefe. (Bryan Cox)

F/SGT J.S. McARTHUR
Oaro
14 SQUADRON

F/L T.R.F. JOHNSON
Auckland
16 SQUADRON

F/O G. RANDELL
Auckland
16 SQUADRON

F/SGT R.W. ALBRECHT
Palmerston North
16 SQUADRON

soldier he was!" said Fujita. "I would like to pray for his soul on his grave."

A newspaper article about the search for Keefe's next of kin appeared in the **New Zealand Sunday News.** On that same day Minoru Fujita received a surprise long distance telephone call from Auckland, New Zealand. The caller was John O'Keefe, the flyer's older brother. A retired college instructor, he had also served with the RNZAF, but did his military service with a night fighter unit over Europe. It was learned that Keefe's widow had since remarried and her privacy was respected.

On March 8, 1988, Mr. and Mrs. Fujita visited the New Zealand Military Cemetery at Noumea, New Caledonia

Padre Roland Hart conducts services for the eight pilots who did not return on January 15, 1945. (Bryan Cox)

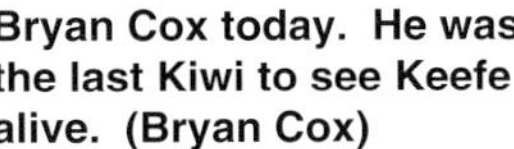
Bryan Cox today. He was the last Kiwi to see Keefe alive. (Bryan Cox)

Minoru Fujita prays for the soul of Frank Keefe at his grave at the New Zealand Military Cemetary on New Caledonia.

Minoru Fujita fulfilled his long quest to meet Frank Keefe's next of kin to tell him what a brave soldier he was. Left to right: Mr. and Mrs. John O'Keefe, Mrs. Fujita, Mrs. Cox, Bryan Cox, and Minoru Fujita.

where he placed flowers and prayed on the grave of Flight Lieutenant Keefe. They departed for Auckland where they met John O'Keefe, his wife, and Bryan Cox, the last Kiwi to see Keefe alive. The Fujitas stayed with the O'Keefes for a week. "They treated me like one of the family," said Fujita graciously of his host.

The O'Keefes now live in Australia. Bryan Cox runs his own flying school and resides in Papakura, New Zealand. In 1987, he authored a book entitled **Too Young to Die - The Story of a New Zealand Fighter Pilot in WWII.** A good natured fellow with a great sense of humor, Cox writes, "...we have just secured a contract to train Indonesian pilots for their airlines, so I should not run out of part time employment next year - I need the money."

Minoru Fujita, now 75 years old, is a retired gardener. He has gained international recognition in the field of tanka (Japanese poetry), and has been invited to the Imperial Palace in Tokyo on three occasions to read his works before the Emperor and court, an unprecedented honor. He has also been cited by the U.S. Congress. Mr. Fujita resides near Los Angeles having moved to California in 1953.

Minoru Fujita at home. A framed photo of Keefe and a miniature New Zealand flag pay homage to the fallen Kiwi.

SUCH A HANDSOME YOUNG MAN

The Hornet launches Hellcats of VBF-17 for a strike on the mainland. (Credit: National Archives via Charles Graham.)

"He was such a handsome young man," recalled eighty-two year old retired nurse Mayumi Shirakata in 1979, reminiscing on the day she saved the life of a captured American fighter pilot.

American Navy aircraft had laid waste to Tokyo and surrounding areas during the great carrier raids of February 16-17, 1945. The armada then shifted their focus south. Enemy airfields had to be neutralized in preparation for storming Okinawa the following month, and it was from these bases that the Kamikazes would sortie on their one way suicide missions. Task Force 58 commenced operations over Japan's Southern Islands on March 18, 1945.

In the early morning hours of March 19, 1945, the pilots of VBF-17 aboard the carrier **Hornet**, bounded out of their bunks and into their flight gear. Today was the "big one". But for Lieutenant (jg) Forrest McCormick, the day got off to a bad start; he was late for breakfast and when he arrived in the mess hall there was nothing left but cold scrambled eggs. He quickly ate and went topside to find his buddies already boarding their aircraft. At 0618, the first Hellcat roared off the deck, bound for the Kure Naval Base area.

Twenty F6Fs, led by Lieutenant Edwin S. Conant, executive officer of the unit, made their way to the staging area to join sixteen **Bennington** Hellcats. The plan was to sweep the airfields on Shikoku and Honshu at Iwakuni, Matsuyama, and Kure. They had an hour to clear the air of any fighter opposition. A second wave of aircraft would follow to destroy the warships anchored in Kure Harbor. By the time the **Hornet** group reached the staging area, the other group had already departed. Miffed at being stood up, they set course for the primary and proceeded on their way.

Unknown to the Americans who were sailing in through the beautiful dawn sky, the Japanese were preparing to extract a terrible toll. The newly formed 343rd Kokutai, an elite naval fighter group, was looking forward to this contest. It had been raised by Captain Minoru Genda, a top naval strategist and the master mind behind the Pearl Harbor attack. Formed in December 1944, the unit was equipped with the new Shiden-Kai (George) fighter. Genda combed all the air units in his quest to assemble his "killer elite". The 343rd had the highest concentration of "veterans" of any Japanese naval air group. In many respects, the 343rd resembled the famous German Luftwaffe's JV-44 ("Squadron of Experts"), an elite jet fighter squadron led by the brilliant General Adolf Galland.

Anticipating an aerial assault that morning, Captain Genda scrambled three squadrons to meet the enemy head-on. Their espirit de corps was very high and each pilot, spoiling for a fight, looked forward to the contest. Squadron 301 was ordered to Kure while thirty-three fighters of the 407th and the 701st probed the Inland Sea area off the coast of Shikoku Island.

VBF-17 passed over the western side of Shikoku and was approximately six miles northwest of the Island when the enemy was spotted. At almost the same instant, the Japanese tallyhoed the Americans. Lieutenant Yoshishige Hiyashi, commanding sixteen Georges (the entire division of the 407th), ordered a 180 degree turn to get to the rear of the American formation. Lieutenant Conant wasn't going to stand for that and ordered his men to make a 180 degree turn to meet the Japanese head-on. The sky was about to explode.

Lieutenant (jg) Forrest McCormick of VBF-17

Lieutenant (jg) Forrest McCormick eventually found himself in trouble. He had made four passes on the Georges and driven them off the tail of his comrade when his radio was knocked out. The sky was full of twisting and smoking aircraft and McCormick suddenly found himself zooming up underneath the tail of a George. The Japanese failed to take evasive action and was flying level, with no idea that a Hellcat was sitting on his tail. At point blank range, McCormick didn't need to use his gunsight.

"I've got you now," he thought as he pressed the gun button. His first victory was going to be an easy one.

The deafening silence of his six .50s stunned him. Nothing! McCormick was so close now he could shear off the George's tail with his propeller. Panic gripped him. Frantically he struggled to recharge his guns, not knowing if they had jammed or were out of ammunition.

Before he could activate the guns his Hellcat was attacked by aircraft from Lieutenant Goro Ichimura's division, the wild dogfight over Shikoku being witnessed from the ground by farmers and villagers near the hamlet of Hirota.

A thunderous roar and a series of explosions shook McCormick's fighter as it was hit from behind. The enemy's 20mm cannon shells had found their mark. They exploded against his armored seat, spewing jagged shrapnel all over the cramped cockpit. He made a violent 180 degree turn to the left but the shells kept slamming into him. The George pilot had him boresighted. Instinctively, he threw up his arms to shield his face. Shrapnel cut deeply into his left arm and elbow. Then his fuel tank exploded. Angry red flames shot up in front of him. "No, no, no!" thought McCormick. "This can't be happening to me!"

The villagers suddenly pointed to the sky. "A parachute!" they shouted. Forrest McCormick had bailed out of his burning aircraft at 10,000 feet. He drifted serenely down into the rugged pine mountains. The villagers quickly organized a searching party and set off, armed with old shotguns, sticks, and pitchforks.

The dogfights drifted away. So fierce was this combat, six pilots from VBF-17 were missing.* They claimed twenty-five victories and nine probables. The 407th's claims are unknown, but they also lost six pilots.

Leading Airman Yoichi Saiki (407 Squadron) was among the Japanese defenders killed by VBF-17 Hellcats after he shot one down on March 19, 1945.

Shiden-Kai (George) fighters of the 407th Squadron on intercep-tion course with VBF-17 Hellcats. The white diagonal fuselage stripes denote the aircraft of Lieutenant Yoshishige Hayashi. (Depiction by Shori Tanaka)

Forrest McCormick recalled his capture:

"As soon as I landed, I pulled out my first aid kit from my backpack and began to dress my wounds. About half an hour later, a party of ten to a dozen men came up the slope. One of them approached cautiously and gestured for me to surrender my weapon but I was unarmed. In my haste to take off that morning I had forgotten my revolver. I had my left arm in a sling and gestured back that I was unarmed. When they were convinced, I was quickly surrounded and marched down the slope to a truck. I received a few blows to my head."

There was excitement in the air. The tall, lanky American was taken off the truck and paraded down Hirota's main street. Anxious villagers pushed and shoved to get a glimpse of the hated enemy. Standing six feet three, he towered over the Japanese. For many of them, this was the first Caucasian they had ever seen. A man rushed up to McCormick, pen and paper in hand, and asked for his name and serial number.

The villagers' collective anger began to swell. Hirota Village was, in the prewar days, a poor farming community. Four years of war had brought even more poverty, hunger, and misery. And for the moment, it seemed, it was all McCormick's fault.

"Kill him!" came a frenzied shout from a man in the crowd. "Beat him," cried another. Others started to join in. The mood was getting ugly. McCormick knew he was in serious trouble.

Mayumi Shirakata, a nurse in the village, had been informed by a neighbor that an American plane had been shot down and that the captured pilot had arrived in the village. She walked out to the street to investigate.

Dr. Sadao Shirakata, who administered to McCormick's wounds, was the physician for the poor farming village of Hirota.

Haruko (Shirakata) Mihara (left), NHK-TV reporter, retired nurse Mayumi Shirakata, and author, 1980.

"The American pilot was around twenty years old," recalled the nurse. "The people were very excited and they were going to hit him with sticks."

Mrs. Shirakata pushed her way toward the hapless American amid loud cries for retribution. She tried to protect the bewildered pilot from the crowd and shouted, "Stop it! Stop it, all of you! This young man may have parents who are surely worrying about him. We have also sent our sons to war. Please imagine your sons in his situation. He is also fighting for the sake of his country. He is blameless. He is hurt and needs help. You must not hurt him. Don't you dare lay a hand on him!"

Stung by the courageous woman's vociferous defense of the injured pilot, the mob grew silent and drew back. Mrs. Shirakata took the pilot to her husband's clinic.

"On this day my husband had many patients, but he made them wait and took care of the pilot," recalled Mrs. Shirakata. "My husband took a long time to take care of him and finally applied bandages fully. He was shivering with pain.

Haruko Shirakata, their shy twelve year old daughter, stood by and gazed at the pilot. She recalled, "About fifty or sixty villagers surrounded the pilot. They were wildly excited. Amongst them he looked queer, strange and somehow beautiful. Here and there his clothes were torn out and stained of blood. I remember he was walking lamely. Soon our hospital was full of villagers. When he went into the hospital (my house), stones were thrown at him and the window was damaged. It was a terrible situation. I cannot forget the time when I watched him and our eyes met. His eyes were light green or light blue and very beautiful, sad and weak. I thought he was nineteen years old or so. I felt pity at the sight of his neck [wound]. How miserable the war was."

McCormick remembered the little girl in the clinic. "I thought it was strange that of all the people in the office, this one little girl came up and watched and nothing was said to her. She must have been their daughter."

After medical treatment McCormick was taken to a nearby house where he laid down on the matted floor. Soldiers came in the late afternoon to take him away. As a security measure the American prisoner was forced to wear welder's goggles. As he was being shoved onto the back of a flatbed truck, Mrs. Shirakata watched pensively. She felt certain that he would be executed like so many captured fliers. The Kempei-Tai (military police) were so harsh in treating captured airmen. There was nothing more she could do for him, so she said a little prayer.

"From the military installation the next morning, I was moved with about a half dozen other prisoners to a train where I passed out due to the pain," said McCormick. "Later, I was forced to walk off the train, then boarded a boat which took us across the strait to where I believed was Kure."

The American prisoners included McCormick and two others from his squadron who had been shot down in the same dogfight. They were interrogated and thrown into a cell which had several Japanese prisoners. "I didn't get the feeling that this was a POW prison," recalled McCormick. "It seemed like a regular prison. I guess that they had problems of their own. I was shoved around, but there was no torture. The guards did, however, use their bamboo sticks quite freely at the slightest irritation."

McCormick finally landed in Ofuna POW Camp, near Tokyo. Toward the end of the war, B-29s dropped their payload close to the camp and damaged some of the compound. He hid out in the camp with several other prisoners, away from the damaged buildings. Several B-29 sergeants thought about making their escape, but McCormick was in no physical condition to do so. Things really took a turn for the worse when the atomic bomb was dropped, but he managed to hang on.

The war finally ended on August 15, 1945, four days after McCormick's twenty-fourth birthday. The prison diet had reduced his weight from 170 pounds to about a hundred. A week later he boarded a hospital ship and was on his way home.

As the years passed, everyone forgot about the quiet auburn-haired son of a minister - except for the Shirakatas in Hirota Village. It wasn't until 1979 that Mrs. Shirakata told her story to a local television news reporter. "'McCormick', such a difficult name to pronounce. It's strange that I would remember it all these years," she mused.

A check with the Naval Historical Center in Washington, D.C. confirmed that a Lieutenant (jg) Forrest McCormick of VBF-17 was missing in action on March 19, 1945 over Shikoku. Captain Marshall U. Beebe (Ret.), former skipper of the outfit got the word out, and through the efforts of his comrades, located the former POW in Enid, Oklahoma. He had retired from the service in 1946, married a year later, and worked on his father-in-law's ranch for about five years. He went back to school and was later employed by the U.S. Post Office.

When Mrs. Shirakata was informed that McCormick was alive and well, she was overjoyed. "I prayed for him for so many years," she said. "I'm so happy to hear that he survived. I would like to meet him some day. He was such a handsome young man."

McCormick sent word to Mrs. Shirakata, thanking her for taking care of him. Dr. Sadao Shirakata, aged ninety-two, passed away two weeks after McCormick was located. He was very ill and deaf at the time and never learned of the good news.

Sadly, Forrest McCormick passed away on November 21, 1989 without ever having visited the nurse who saved his life.

* Of the six VBF-17 pilots downed, three were killed in action and three survived as prisoners of war: Lt. Charles F. Weiss (POW), Lt. (jg) Forrest McCormick (POW), Ens. Edwin W. Matthews (POW), Lt. Strother T. Kipp (MIA), Lt. R.W. Karr (MIA), Ens. H.L. Hannah (MIA)

Forrest McCormick (center) being interviewed by a Japanese TV reporter as Captain Marshall U. Beebe looks on. Beebe commanded VF-17 in 1945 and was instrumental in locating McCormick. Beebe, respected leader, ace, and test pilot, passed away in March 1991.

MUSTANGS OVER SHANGHAI

First Lieutenant Edward J. Bollen was bored. The 23rd Fighter Group was witnessing little action in March 1945. A mixture of bad weather and lack of fuel had grounded most of the P-51s. Even when missions were flown, few enemy aircraft were encountered and the Mustang jocks had to be content with harassing enemy troops and strafing installations. Photo recon missions added very little excitement. But that would all change on April 2, 1945.

Mission 17 materialized to relieve the boredom. A coordinated attack on four airfields in the Shanghai area involving Mustangs from the 75th and 76th Fighter Squadrons, led by Lieutenant Colonel Ed Rector of the 23rd Fighter Group.

Ed Bollen, then with the 75th Fighter Squadron, recalls the events of this memorable day: "Takeoff was uneventful and we headed out on course. It would be more than two hours to the target area which gave us plenty of time to think about all those Zeros waiting for us. To make matters worse, we had seven aircraft abort the mission which then increased the odds even greater on the side of the bad guys. One big thing in our favor was the Japanese were not accustomed to fighter strikes in the Shanghai area and, in addition, we were coming quite early in the morning."

The "bad guys" that Bollen alluded to was the Japanese Navy's 256th Kokutai. Organized at Lunghwa Airfield on February 1, 1944, its main duties were air defense over the Shanghai region and advanced training for young pilots. This group contributed Zero fighters in the Philippines Campaign and suffered horrendous losses. By April 1945 there were less than two dozen fighters on hand and their combat success had been dismal. It was this unit that was depicted in the hit movie, **Empire of the Sun**.

"We approached Shanghai at about ten thousand feet," said Bollen, "and when about twenty miles out started a high speed descent. At this time, the four groups split with each going to their assigned airfield. Our group headed for Lunghwa with only five aircraft. A flight of three led by Captain Forrest (Pappy) Parham with Lieutenant Jack Quinn and Lieutenant Don King were to strafe the airfield while Captain Ernest Harper (our operations officer) and I flew top cover to protect them from any fighters that may be airborne. The flight of three got down to tree top level and Harper and I leveled about 3,000 feet. When we were four miles out, I spotted a fighter over the airfield at about 4,000 feet and climbing in a circle to the left. I called him out to Harper and we started an immediate climb towards it."

Lieutenant Masatake Hayasaki had just taken off from Lunghwa Airfield at 1015. The thirty-three year old pilot began circling the airfield, putting the Raiden ("Jack") through its paces. The new aircraft had just arrived in the unit. This was its first test flight. Bad timing.

"We were headed north and I was on the right side of Harper," recalls Bollen. "We pulled in behind him while still on a northerly course with Harper at the Jap's altitude while I moved up about another 500 feet. Harper at this

Lunghwa Airfield, home base of the 256th "Thunder Corps". This was the Japanese airfield depicted in the movie Empire of the Sun. (Ed Bollen)

Lieutenant Masatake Hayasaki with A6M2 Type 21 Zeros of the 256th Kokutai "Thunder Corps". (Hayasaki family.)

time was directly behind him and I was about 1,000 feet to the right.

"The Japanese pilot must have seen Harper about the time he got into range for he made an immediate hard turn to the left causing Harper to overshoot the turn, not being able to pull any lead on the aircraft. I started a diving turn to the left pulling into range about the time he had completed 180 degrees of turn. I was now on a westerly heading which put me up-sun from him. This placed me in a ninety degree deflection shot and in relation to his aircraft, I was aiming straight down into his cockpit. I pulled the proper lead and fired three short bursts. All three hit in and around the cockpit area. We were using API (armor piercing incendiary) ammunition which gave little flashes of light when they hit. As I completed the three bursts, I was in so close that I had to break off the pass and I pulled into a steep climb to get into position for another attack. As I climbed, I lowered my left wing to see what he was doing and saw that I had shot his left wing off at the root and that he had bailed out. His chute worked as advertised and he floated down not more than a mile from the field. While we searched around for more aircraft, the other three were busy shooting up aircraft which hadn't got off the ground."

The mission resulted in the following credits: Bollen - one aircraft destroyed in the air; Lieutenant Gordon C. Berven - one Betty bomber destroyed on the ground; Lieutenant Ernest Harper, Jr. - one four engined seaplane destroyed on the ground; and Lieutenant Donald E. King - one single-engined aircraft damaged on the ground.

The official Japanese record stated that one Raiden took off after intruders. Three minutes later, eight P-51s strafed the airfield at very low altitude. The Raiden intercepted the enemy aircraft, but was hit and dove to the ground at 1025, about two kilometers from base and the pilot was killed. Japanese losses amounted to one Raiden in the air, one Zero trainer and a flying boat burned by

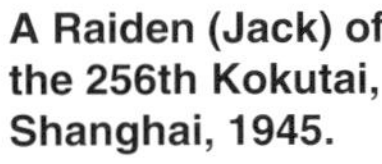
A Raiden (Jack) of the 256th Kokutai, Shanghai, 1945.

P-51Ds of the 75th Fighter Squadron. (Ed Bollen)

strafing attacks, plus four more aircraft damaged on the ground. Anti-aircraft on the airfield failed to bring down the enemy aircraft.

A Shanghai newspaper, **Shen Bao**, reported the April 2nd attack in this fashion:

"On the morning of April 2nd, about ten enemy planes (P-51s) divided into two groups, descended to twenty feet above the ground and opened fire. The group at southwest Shanghai shot at civilian houses located at Chan Jian Chao Town and Pan Jian Liang. About ten Chinese were killed and wounded. When the enemy planes were only fifteen feet high above the ground the old and the young were running away. Knowing that they were civilians the enemy still strafed them. The non-moralistic behavior made the people irritated. The Japanese forces opened fire at those planes, one of which was hit. The canopy and auxiliary fuel tank flew off and it finally crashed into the Su Zhou Riverbank. The nearby civilians who were on the scene clapped and cheered. There were three planes shot down and another four were hit. The rest all left."

"Notice that they didn't mention the Jack I shot down," said Ed Bollen, "nor the other aircraft destroyed. We didn't strafe anything but the airfields."

The Chinese news, obviously propaganda, reported that three aircraft were shot down. Actually, it was close to the truth. Major Slocumb, Captain Parham and Lieutenants Quinn and King were downed by ground fire and bailed out. All were met by friendly Chinese when they touched down and eventually returned to the squadron. Major Clyde Slocumb, leading the 75th Fighter Squadron that day, had a harrowing experience.

He was strafing Kiangwan Airfield when he took hits and parachuted to the ground across Huangpu River. "Two Chinese came running just as I hit the ground," he recalls. "One had a hoe in his hands. I didn't know whether he was going to hit me or help me. He helped me dig a hole to bury the parachute, then he helped me run as fast as I could. I had been hit in the left knee by shrapnel, and it was bleeding heavily. I continued to run as fast as possible and when I couldn't go any more, they got me a bicycle to ride. After riding as long as I could, I couldn't do that any more and they put me in a wheelbarrow and rolled me around from place to place."

Major Slocumb returned after forty-three days of evasion and credits the Chinese with saving his life. "I felt so close to the people who did so much for me when I was absolutely helpless," he says. "It's something that draws people together forever."

In 1981 Mr. Huang Ming-Chu of Shanghai, one of the two Chinese who aided him when he touched down, located Slocumb through the help of the Washington Post and Anna Chennault, widow of the late General Claire

Major Clyde Slocum (left) and Captain Forrest Parham on their way back from the April 2, 1945 mission to Shanghai. (Ed Bollen)

Ed Bollen and his crew chief, William Heath. "Eadie Mae" was named after his wife. (Ed Bollen)

Chennault, founder of the famous “Flying Tigers”. The retired USAF Colonel, residing in Georgia, was very happy to renew the old friendship.

Lieutenant Bollen had his first confirmed victory - his only one for the war - and painted a “meatball” on the side of his faithful “Eadie Mae” (named after his wife). As he was to learn years later, the meatball had a name attached to it - Masatake Hayasaki.

Lieutenant Hayasaki was a family man. His wife Miki (twenty-eight years old) and their two children (a boy, age nine and a daughter, age six) had dearly missed him. His loss was a terrible blow to the family and his wife struggled for many years after the war to raise their two children. She became a school teacher. Both the Hiyasaki children, now married, are in the banking business. Her husband’s remains were returned to Nagasaki.

On November 1, 1989, Ed Bollen wrote to Mrs. Miki Hayasaki, the widow of the pilot he shot down over Lunghwa Airfield. His letter in part read, “In researching the records, I had hoped to find that Masatake had survived the war and that we could meet again as friends.

Lieutenant Hayasaki (right) with a comrade. Note the aerial training camera mounted on the wing. (Hayasaki family)

I am sure that at the time of our combat mission over Shanghai, neither of us had any desire to kill the other but were doing our duty to our countries in that unfortunate war...I again want to express my sorrow for the death of your husband and ask for forgiveness from you and your family. I hope this letter finds you all in the best of health and may God bless you and your children and grandchildren.”

A while after posting the letter, Ed Bollen received a warm response from Mrs. Hayasaki’s son. This came as a relief to the former Mustang pilot, who had wondered if he would ever hear from the family. Ed now resides in Sewickley, Pennsylvania.

Down on the farm. Ed Bollen as he is today.

COMPASSION AND SAVAGERY

P-51D Mustangs of the 47th Ftr Sq., 15th Ftr Grp. enroute to Honshu from Iwo Jima.

"I want to become a fighter ace," Robert Silvio Scamara would tell his friends as a kid growing up in the Depression Era. He read about the famous flying aces of World War I in pulp magazines and vowed to join their ranks. Their daring exploits thrilled the youngster to no end. When World War II came around he was ready. The two year college requirement for the Air Corps had been dropped. Fresh out of high school, he was accepted into the service on October 28, 1942.

Bob Scamara grew up in San Luis Obispo, California, right along the Pacific coast. John V. (Jack) Scanlan, soon to become Scamara's squadron mate, hailed from Louisville, Kentucky. World War II was fought and won by "kids" like Scamara and Scanlan. However, they did not share in the glories of those illustrious comrades who became aces by shooting down five or more enemy planes.

By the summer of 1945, the Japanese were defeated but hadn't called it a war. They were hoarding their remaining aircraft for the one last counterattack against the anticipated invasion of Japan. Most of the Japanese planes encountered by American pilots were considered "target practice", a preferred diversion from dangerous strafing jobs.

On June 23, 1945 at 0938, P-51s from the 47th Fighter Squadron began taking off from their base on Iwo Jima from which they had been attacking Japan since early April. The mission was to lay havoc to Shimodate Airfield, a bomber base northeast of Tokyo.

Unfortunately this placed the Mustangs within easy reach of the 601 Kokutai, then based to the southwest at Hyakurigahara Airfield. The 601st was the most powerful air group operating in all of central Japan. They had over a hundred Zeros plus a number of Shiden (George) fighters. (See map, page 92.)

Second Lieutenants Bob Scamara and Jack Scanlan teamed up for the very long range mission to the hostile mainland. "He had light brown hair and was tall and thin," recalled Scamara of his wingman. "We often kidded him about how baggy his flight suit fit him. To get the right length the rest of the suit had to be too big."

The six flights were led by Lieutenant Colonel Julian E. Thomas, CO of the 15th Fighter Group. Scamara and Scanlan belonged to Yellow Flight, led by First Lieutenant Harold Baccus. They sailed over their departure point at 1300. After turning toward the primary target they saw enemy aircraft. The squadron made their way toward Kasumigaura (a large naval airfield) and were attacked by seventeen fighters. Although initially identified as Franks (JAAF Type 84 fighters) the enemy aircraft were most certainly Navy Shidens and Zeros from the 601st.

"All at once there was a lot of excited radio chatter with everyone calling out bogies," recalls Scamara. "I saw streaks of light in front of me and finally came to my senses and realized there were tracers coming from behind."

He did some wild maneuvering with Scanlan glued to his wings. In a vicious ten minute dogfight the Mustang flights became widely separated. Isolated from the rest of the Group, Scamara and Scanlan decided to make their way toward their rally point. As they raced back over Kasumigaura Lake they were spotted by the enemy.

Scamara sent two of them plunging down into the lake bottom. However, like angry hornets, the Japanese swarmed about them and both Americans were in danger of being overwhelmed. They were trying to work their way south with a swarm of enemy aircraft right behind them. "After I rolled out of a turn and could see Jack, it was a little late. There were two Japs sneaking up on his tail that he couldn't see. I called him on the radio to move but he didn't do a thing. Meanwhile, I was heading for him yelling into the radio for him to do something - anything, but he just flew on straight and level."

Scamara was horrified, seeing clearly that Jack Scanlan was hit. His wing was on fire cooking off machine gun ammo like fireworks.

Captain Yasumasa Miyasaka of the Imperial Army looked up at the swirling air battle. He had been directing his men in the digging of underground fortifications near the mountains of Iioka near Kujukurihama Beach (Chiba Prefecture). He recalls the unusual events of that day.

Capt. Yasumasa Miyasaka of the Imperial Army, March 1945.

Bob Scamara, Bellows Field, Oahu, Dec., 1944.

John V. "Jack" Scanlan as a newly commissioned 2nd Lt. fresh from flight training.

"I happened to notice one plane falling, so we were all very excited and glad to see what we thought was an enemy plane. But it was a Japanese fighter plane and we were very discouraged. Then later on one plane was falling again. It flew over us at low altitude trailing smoke and a white parachute opened. Several of my men ran to the potato field yelling that an enemy pilot was coming down."

Scamara tried to protect his wingman as he descended. Only two of his guns were working. He made a head-on exchange with the enemy but soon his ammo was exhausted. He could do no more for Scanlan and was forced to leave the area at full throttle. Once back on Iwo Jima gun camera film gave evidence of the ferocity of Scamara's battle. He received credit for the destruction of three enemy aircraft and seven damaged.

Jack Scanlan landed roughly in a potato field bleeding heavily in three places and moaning in pain. Miyasaka's men were already on top of the hapless American and shouted to kill him with bayonets and bamboo spears. The captain arrived just in time.

He took immediate charge of the prisoner and ordered his men back. He cut up pieces of parachute to stem the bleeding. Scanlan was in agony and kept pleading to Miyasaka. "Although I didn't understand English I'm sure he was saying 'please help me' repeatedly," recalls Miyasaka. "My men rummaged through his pockets and found some papers that they promptly tore up in anger and scattered on the ground. I was too busy tending to the American."

His men were angry. They wanted to know why they couldn't execute the enemy pilot. Miyasaka was irritated. The badly wounded American was not a threat and completely at their mercy.

A truck came and took Scanlan away. Captain Miyasaka made a full report of the incident to his commander. The commander remained silent until Miyasaka was finished, then responded, "I understand."

Miyasaka was relieved that his commander did not show any negative attitude toward his handling of the situation. "Several days later I was told by an official of the hospital that the wounded American pilot was alive," said Miyasaki. But it was a lie and he wouldn't know the truth until forty-six years later.

Jack Scanlan arrived at the Army's 152nd Divisional Headquarters at Sawara-Machi. The intelligence officer, Captain Yoshinaga Suzuki, tried to speak to the injured pilot but Scanlan could not understand his English. After writing his name on a piece of paper, he collapsed. Medical Officer Wakano ordered his men to place the flier on a bed. At 1630, a mob started to form outside the building demanding custody of Scanlan.

Major Yoshio Shingo, who was visiting the 152nd Division, urged Colonel Chiyoshi Shimoda to turn the wounded prisoner over to the civilians. Said Shingo to Shimoda, "It is just a custom to take revenge on captives. They do that everywhere. I saw people hitting prisoners at Yasukuni Shrine."

Shimoda responded, "Is that so?" He barked his order to Captain Suzuki, "Take him out."

A mob of over a dozen then beat the helpless flier to death.

At war crimes trials held in Tokyo in 1948 Colonel Chiyoshi Shimoda received forty years imprisonment at hard labor. Major Yoshio Shingo was convicted for urging Shimoda to turn Scanlan over to the civilians. He received five years imprisonment. Other participants received one and five year prison terms and eight were acquitted. The lenient sentences outraged Catherine Scanlan, the boy's mother and the rest of the clan. They have remained bitter to this day. Jack Scanlan's remains were recovered and brought home.

In a letter dated March 10, 1991, Bob Scamara wrote, "If indeed that was Scanlan that Mr. Miyasaka saved, I would sure like to offer my sincere thanks for the humanitarian treatment he extended to him or to whoever it was. It is nice to know there were still some Japanese people with such feeling after all they had been subjected to during the war. His interest and concern to trace the American pilot is also to be commended."

Bob Scamara ended the war with four confirmed victories and seven damaged - just one victory short of realizing his boyhood dream of becoming an "ace". He says that Jack Scanlan shot down an enemy plane in his last fight for which he was never given credit. "I definitely saw Jack shoot down a plane but things were so hot and heavy, I couldn't remember any of the details. This could be the Japanese plane Mr. Miyasaka witnessed prior to Scanlan's parachute descent," he remarked.

Bob Scamara went back to school after the war and graduated with a degree in Aeronautical Engineering from Cal Poly in 1949. He started working for the Division of Highways in 1950, and after thirty-seven years retired in 1987. He now resides in the San Luis Obispo area.

As for Yasumasa Miyasaka, now seventy-two and president of a sake brewery in Nagano City, he was very angry to learn about the fate of Jack Scanlan. He remarked that there was simply no excuse for his barbaric treatment and death. If and when Mr. Miyasaka visits the United States he has vowed to visit Arlington Natonal Cemetary and quietly pay his respects to Jack Scanlan.

Bob Scamara today.

Yasumasa Miyasaka today, with his wife. His curiosity about the Mustang pilot he saved on June 23, 1945 led to this story.

DRAGON SLAYER

"B-29!"

No other term struck such terror in the hearts of the Japanese public during World War II than this single, most hated name. It was then only natural that the people would come to respect and admire those brave pilots who risked their lives to slay the mighty "flying dragons". One of the best known "dragon slayers" of the Japanese Army Air Force was Captain Isamu Kashiide, called "The King of B-29 Killers".

Kashiide was born in 1915 in Niigata Prefecture, Honshu, one of the poorest and least developed regions of Japan. Even as a youth, he had dreams of becoming a pilot, entered the Army flight training program in 1934 and graduated in November 1935. He was posted to the Army's 1st Air Regiment.

When the China War broke out, he was sent to Northern China in 1938, but saw no combat until September 1939. A border dispute between Outer Mongolia (backed by the Soviets) and Japanese dominated Manchuria led to the Nomohan (Khalkan Gol) Incident. This undeclared war was of very short duration, and the Russians inflicted a humiliating defeat that cost the Japanese 18,000 casualties, mostly on the ground. However, the Japanese crushed the Soviets in the air. Kashiide, flying the standard Type 27 fighter, shot down two Soviet fighters in his baptism of fire. He claimed another five I-15 and I-16 fighters before the conclusion of the campaign.

Kashiide was reassigned to the 4th Army Sentai (air group) in the Spring of 1940 and was stationed in Taiwan. When the Pacific War started, he participated in the Philippines action but claimed no victories. His unit returned to Japan and was based at Kozuki Airfield in Southern Honshu.

The first B-29 raid on the sacred Japanese homeland was flown by sixty-eight Superfortresses from bases deep in China, on the night of June 15/16, 1944. Their target was the Imperial Iron and Steel Works at Yawata, on the northern coast of Kyushu. This mission marked the debut of the home defense fighter groups, primarily Kashiide's unit.

The 4th Sentai was equipped with the Ki-45 "Toryu" (Dragon Slayer), a twin-engined fighter that had initially failed in its intended role as long range escort/interceptor and was then pressed into service as a nightfighter. It carried a two man crew (pilot and rear gunner observer), and the 4th Sentai's Ki-45s were armed with a 37mm anti-tank cannon. It was given the Allied code name "Nick".

Captain Isamu Kashiide

Kashiide recalls his first combat with the massive B-29, "I was flying over the industrial area of Northern Kyushu when our commander radioed the message, 'Enemy planes invading an important area. Every flight attack!' Simultaneously, ground searchlights lit up the sky. Then, I sighted the enemy four engined bomber. I was scared. It was known that the B-29 was a huge plane,

View from nose of a B-29 approaching Tokyo. The cone of Mt. Fuji served as a landmark. January 1945. (Credit: USAF)

but when I saw my opponent it was much larger than I had ever expected. There was no question that when compared to the B-17, the B-29 was the Superfortress. The figure that appeared in the searchlights made me think of it as a great whale in the ocean. I was astounded by its size."

The Dragon Slayer was positioned for a head-on attack. Sergeant Tanabe, Kashiide's observer, yelled into the communication tube, "Instructor, I rely on you."

The 37 mm cannon roared and Kashiide dropped the plane down. Fear, tension, and adrenaline were high and served to confuse Kashiide in the darkness. He believed he struck the bomber in the left wing. "Got it," he shouted.

The B-29 crews reported that sixteen enemy aircraft made weak, ineffectual attacks that night, including three by twin engined fighters. Only twelve passes were pressed to within 500 yards and only five aircraft opened fire. Although Kashiide claimed a victory and a probable, no B-29s were hit and no Japanese fighters were claimed by bomber gunners. In the wild confusion of their first combat, the Japanese claimed five B-29s destroyed and another five damaged.

August 20, 1944 marked one of the first B-29 daylight raids over Japan when a second try at reducing the Yawata Iron and Steel Works to rubble was attempted by the 40th, 444th, 462nd, and the 468th Bomb Groups. Seventy-five B-29s took off from their Chinese bases, but six aborted and two others went down enroute. Sixty-one bombed Yawata and six hit other targets. As the formation reached between 20 to 26,000 feet, it was met with heavy flak and a horde of enemy fighters. For half an hour, the Japanese assaulted the Superforts, coming in from the front and below.

First Lieutenant Kashiide executed his favorite maneuver - a head-on charge into the enemy formation. To his right was Sergeant Shigeo Nobe of the 3rd Squadron with Sgt. Denzo Takagi as observer. Nobe made a spontaneous decision to ram and radioed his intentions to Kashiide, his flight leader. "I will do it, instructor!" yelled Nobe over the radio.

"No, don't be hasty," shot back Kashiide.

Nobe was on a collision course with the aircraft of Colonel Robert Clinkscales. Leading a four plane diamond formation of the 794th, Clinkscales was the pilot of GERTRUDE C. named after his mother. He had just released his bombs when a twin-engined fighter suddenly

Pilots of the 4th Sentai at Kozuki, Spring 1944. Sitting in foreground, left to right: Sergeant Uchida, Lieutenant Kashiide, and Sergeant Nobe.

Four 468th Group pilots who were on the August 20, 1944 mission to Yawata. Left to right: Colonel James V. Edmundson, Colonel Robert Clinkscales holding Sally, Major Donald Humphrey, and Major James Van Horn. (Donald Humphrey)

appeared about 50-100 yards in front, approaching at twelve o'clock level. Nobe banked his aircraft to the right and became vertical; his right wing struck the left wing of the Superfort and ripped open the wing tanks.

GERTRUDE C. immediately burst into flames and for a brief moment, the Nick was seen lodged in her wing before both aircraft exploded. The flaming remains of Nobe's aircraft then catapulted over the right wing of Major Donald J. Humphrey's POSTVILLE EXPRESS. In the trail position, immediately behind and below GERTRUDE C., Captain Ornell Stauffer, pilot of CALAMITY SUE, pulled up to avoid the wreckage, but it sheared off his horizontal stabilizer and CALAMITY SUE spun all the way down to the ground. Only one crew member survived from the two B-29s. The other bombers closed ranks and continued on.

The Yawata mission was a day of tragedy for the Americans. Fourteen B-29s were lost and eight were damaged. Although bomber gunners claimed seventeen enemy fighters shot down, there was no rejoicing in the Twentieth Air Force. This was their worst loss record to date.

Despite success by 4th Sentai pilots (they claimed seventeen B-29s downed with eight probables), their only losses (Nobe and Takagi) cut deeply into their hearts. Nobe received a posthumous citation for valor and a song was later written about his brave deed.

Fighting against the B-29 required nerves of steel and a precise method of attack; anything less was suicidal. Kashiide resolved to train his subordinates harder and formulated an attack plan, based upon his experiences.

"'Kashiide Style Combat Techniques' was the name given to my fighting tactics," recalls Kashiide. "Maneuver from within 1,000 meters. The B-29s have thirteen machine guns; in a head-on attack, you will be faced with ten of them. I will always fly in front and I will always be the first to attack. I am showered with tracers every time. Tracers coming toward you in a criss cross pattern are very frightening. I feel that my vision is shot

Postville Express, in a photo taken from Gertrude C. This photo came from a camera found in the wreckage of the Gertrude C.

away in the screen of bullets. It is not a good feeling to have. In such cases, close your eyes and count to three. When you open your eyes, the enemy will be within 200 meters of you. Adjust your sights with 150 - 200 meters from the target. At 100 meters, lower your plane. At 80 meters, fire, then dive your plane quickly - go straight down. At times, I think I will crash against the belly of the bomber. The air current under the B-29 is enormous and very dangerous. If you can't dive fast enough, you will get

Kashiide combs through the wreckage of a B-29 that he has shot down.

The proud crew of Rover Boy Express, 878th Sq., 499th Bomb Grp., as they departed for Saipan. Left to right, back row: Lt. Bob Grace, bombardier, KIA; Lt. Willie Franz, Eng., KIA; Lt. Hap Halloran, navigator, Lt. Jim Edwards, co-pilot, Lt. Ed Smith, AC Commander. Middle row: Guy Knobel, Bob Holliday, KIA; Cecil Laird, KIA; Vito Barbieri, KIA; Tony Lukasicewiz, KIA, John Nicholson. (R.F. Halloran)

caught in the slipstream and your plane will become uncontrollable. You can get shot down by the tail gunner."

"I always aim for the cockpit. If I miss the cockpit, then it may hit the wing or the tail. These are the enemy's three main weak spots. One hit into these areas and the enemy is sure to go down. The enemy's wing will break away under the strain of the air current when damaged by an explosive shell. If the rudder is shot off, the plane will lose control. The speed and direction of your plane and your target must be judged in an instant. Fix your sights, fire, then dive down. This ability is a must!"

"Scratch one dragon." Lieutenant Kashiide in his Kawasaki Ki-45 "Nick", scores a direct hit on Rover Boy Express high over Tokyo on January 27, 1945. (Depiction by Shori Tanaka)

Rover Boy Express, as photographed from another B-29, on fire near Tokyo, Jan 27, 1945. "We had probably all bailed out by now," says Halloran. "We had no power to guns and it was 58 degrees below zero inside." Five crew members survived, six died. (R.F. Halloran)

If the August 20, 1944 mission was the costliest to date, January 27, 1945 was certainly the next toughest. Raymond F "Hap " Halloran, a twenty-two year old navigator aboard ROVER BOY EXPRESS, of the 499th Bomb Group, was making his fifth mission to Japan. The 73rd Bomb Wing put up seventy-six Superforts, but fighter opposition was so intense going into Tokyo, none of the bombers hit the primary target. B-29 crews reported over 900 fighter attacks by an estimated 350 fighters. Japanese Army and Navy fighters swarmed over and through the formations like angry hornets. Some Japanese pilots, not satisfied with their guns, resorted to intentional ramming attacks.

As ROVER BOY EXPRESS flew toward an aircraft factory west of Tokyo, First Lieutenant Kashiide maneuvered his aircraft for his favorite head-on run. He had the enemy clearly in his gunsight and squeezed off a 37mm round. A direct hit! V SQUARE 27 was going down.

Hap Halloran recalls the terror that followed, "They blew off the nose or a good portion of the plexiglass, shot out all the electrical controls, our intercom was out - a lot of smoke in the plane."

Halloran quickly strapped on the parachute he kept stowed under the plotting board. Then, he decided to go back for his lunch of turkey sandwiches and chocolate pudding. The pilot, First Lieutenant E.G. "Snuffy" Smith, was incredulous. "You're crazy! Let's get out of here, we're on fire!" he yelled in Halloran's face. The young navigator reconsidered, took several big bites of his sandwich and jumped. He knew he wasn't going to be eating well again.

Falling like a rock high over Tokyo, Halloran didn't dare open his chute until getting down to a safer altitude lest he freeze to death. The temperature was fifty-seven degrees below zero. One of his boots was torn away. When he finally opened his chute, three fighters made passes as he dangled helplessly. "I waved to them and smiled," he recalled. "They waved, smiled, and pulled off. I think that's a kind of a comradeship between fliers." The native from Cincinnati was captured and endured periodic beatings. He wound up at Omori Prison and became friends with famed Marine Corps Ace, "Pappy" Boyington.

Captain Isamu Kashiide continued to raise havoc against the endless horde of B-29s. On March 27, 1945, he downed three B-29s and damaged three others. In recognition of this and numerous other feats, he was awarded the BUKOSHO - the rare and coveted Army merit badge equivalent in distinction to America's Medal of Honor. (Shown below.)

Top B-29 killers of the 4th Sentai. Back row, lerft to right: Sergeants Shigeo Nobe, two victories by ramming KIA; Hannoshin Nishio, five victories; and Shinji Mori, claims unknown. Front (left to right): Sergeant Minoru Uchida, three victories, KIA; and Lieutenant Isamu Kashiide, 26 victories.

The atomic bombing of Hiroshima on August 6, 1945 hastened the end of the Pacific War. Kashiide was an unsuspecting witness to the first true weapon of mass destruction. While flying on patrol, he was alerted to the presence of three B-29 intruders. As he neared Hiroshima, he was dumbfounded to see a monstrous black mushroom cloud shooting straight into the sky. There was no trace of a once great city. He reported over the radio, "Enemy planes dropped numerous bombs, great damage done." Three days later, he witnessed the aftermath of the atomic bombing of Nagasaki from the air.

Japan's surrender announcement on August 15, 1945 ended the flying career of Captain Isamu Kashiide. By his own reckoning, he destroyed twenty-six B-29s and seven Soviet fighters, bringing his final tally to thirty-three enemy aircraft shot down in aerial combat. Although his claim of twenty-six B-29s is disputed by other pilots and historians, Kashiide was widely known to the public as "The King of B-29 Killers".

Hap Halloran, who was shot down by Kashiide, was fortunate to survive the war. He had gone into captivity weighing 212 pounds and came out at 115. He discovered that four other crewmen of his plane survived the downing, including his commander, E.G. Smith.

On January 27, 1984, at 3:00 P.M., Hap Halloran touched down on a jetliner from San Francisco to Narita International Airport (Japan), almost to the minute he bailed out over Tokyo thirty-nine years previously. He was warmly greeted at the airport by Kaneyuki Kobayashi, one of his former prison camp guards who befriended and aided him during his ordeal.

Why had Halloran, a top official with one of America's biggest freight haulers (Consolidated Freightways) come back to Japan? He replied "...I wanted to end up purging the negative things I remembered about any place. This just happens to be Tokyo. I just wanted

Liberation! "Hap" Halloran (circled), August 29, 1945 at Omori Prison just outside of Tokyo. (R.F. Halloran)

to get things in order, and with that purge, I just thought I'd come back and view it from a positive standpoint."

In 1985, Hap Halloran completed his catharsis by meeting the man who shot him down - Isamu Kashiide. Officials of the American Embassy and former Zero Ace Saburo Sakai worked hard to bring this about. It was a warm and friendly meeting this second time around and both former opponents joked and laughed about their first encounter over Tokyo.

Isamu Kashiide lives in his native Niigata Prefecture and believes that he was very fortunate to survive the war which took the lives of so many of his faithful subordinates. Hap Halloran, semi-retired but always on the go, believes that his fate was in the hands of God. He makes his home in the San Francisco Bay area.

On February 21, 1993, Shori Tanaka, a Tokyo jazz singer, master photographer and a close friend of Halloran, went hunting for V Square 27. He was aided in his search by David Leytze, an American musician living in Tokyo. Information from Japanese military archives and a newspaper article pointed in the direction of a bamboo forest in Chiba Prefecture. A chance mention of the quest to a taxi driver during a ride to the area produced an eyewitness to the crash, an old woman still living near the site.

ROVER BOY EXPRESS had exploded in midair and came down in several places. It set fire to the bamboo forest. After the war, an American investigating team recovered three skeletons and removed all of the wreckage. They left the giant tires which the locals cut up to make sandals. There are most likely small pieces of wreckage there and the two supersleuths plan to go back with metal detectors.

It is only a matter of time before "Hap" Halloran will also go back to visit the final resting place of his B-29 and pay his respects.

U.S. Embassy, September 17, 1985, Tokyo, Japan. Raymond "Hap" Halloran with the man who shot him down, Isamu Kashiide. Saburo Sakai, the legendary Zero pilot (right) assisted in identifying/locating Kashiide.

A Ki-45A1b Toryu, "Nick" of the 4th Sentai. (Depiction by Donald A. Soderlund, Jr.)

THE MAN WHO DID NOT SHOOT DOWN PAPPY BOYINGTON

"I shot down nineteen enemy planes, rammed three times, was shot down twice and parachuted four times," boasts former Zero pilot Masajiro "Mike" Kawato. And did this One Man Air Force also shoot down Marine Corps war hero "Pappy" Boyington as he has proclaimed? After more than fourteen years of claims and counterclaims, it's time to set the record straight.

Masajiro Kawato was born on September 19, 1925 in the small farming village of Takeno, in Kyoto Prefecture, Honshu, Japan. He was the eldest child of Hisaharu and Yaeko Kawato. After completing eight years of public education, he volunteered for naval flight training in August 1941.

Kawato's flying career commenced when he was called up to the Maizuru Naval Barracks on May 1, 1942. On August 1st he was assigned to Iwakuni Naval Air Station for elementary training: classroom studies, basic piloting, and military drill. He progressed to Yatabe Naval Air Base and later trained in the Type 96 fighter (Claude) at Izumi and Tokoshima Air Bases. The Type 96, a relic from the China War, served as a secondary fighter and trainer.

By the time Kawato graduated from flight training on July 27, 1943 Japan was fighting a purely defensive war. After the crushing disaster at Midway in June 1942, pilot training became an assembly line procedure. Many shortcuts were taken in the rush to replace war losses of highly trained pilots and quality suffered.

Battle orders came on September 27, 1943 when Kawato and forty-four other newly graduated members of his class embarked on four transport planes. Refueling at Tinian the next day, they arrived at Truk on October 1st where each pilot was assigned a Zero fighter. They flew their aircraft to the ultimate destination - Rabaul, New Britain. Rabaul had become known as "The Graveyard of Fighter Pilots". On October 10, 1943 Petty Officer Third Class Masajiro Kawato became a member of the 253rd Kokutai (air group). This veteran outfit was based at Tobera Airfield under the leadership of Commander Taro Fukuda. Two of the Navy's top veteran pilots, Warrant Officers Hiroyoshi Nishizawa and Tetsuzo Iwamoto, had served with the unit.

In his postwar writings Kawato has made many extravagant claims to fame which will be analyzed. It should be noted that his original memoir was published in Japan in 1956 under the title **Zero-Sen Rabaul Ni Ari.** It was published by Konnichi-No-Wadai, a small aviation pulp magazine house. Kawato's current book in English (**Flight Into Conquest**, KNI, Inc. Anaheim, CA, 1978) is actually a literal translation of his 1956 memoir. The author writes: "The original manuscript was started in 1976..." It is interesting to note that there is not one mention of an F4U Corsair in his Japanese memoir. The segments dealing with Corsairs and "Pappy" Boyington were added in his English edition.

A boyish looking Masajiro Kawato at Rabaul in 1943.

On October 2, 1943: Kawato claims to have rammed a B-25. This was impossible, he didn't arrive in Rabaul until eight days later.

On October 11, 1943: Claims to have shot down a Corsair in the vicinity of Kokopo, near Rabaul. The F4U didn't make its combat debut over Rabaul until December 17, 1943.

October 15, 1943: Claims a P-38 near Buna, New Guinea. It has been confirmed that Kawato did fly on this mission. Although he claims that twenty-four P-38s and P-40s were shot down, there were no American losses.

On November 2, 1943 the Fifth Air Force bombed Rabaul in support of the landings on Bougainville Island.

Kawato was one of 112 Zero pilots sent up to oppose seventy-eight B-25s and escorting P-38s of the 39th and 80th Fighter Squadrons and the 475th Fighter Group. Kawato's statement that aerial burst bombs were used is confirmed by American records, however, no planes were lost to this ordnance. Kawato claims two P-38s on this date: Nine Lightnings were lost on this raid, of which at least four were shot down by enemy fighters. Kawato also claims that he was attacked by a Corsair which damaged his aircraft. Again, there were no Corsairs involved in this action even though he states that he saw the plane with its bearded pilot blasting away at him just thirty meters behind.

The results of the November 2nd raid were as follows: The Fifth Air Force claimed forty enemy fighters shot down by P-38s and twenty-six more by bomber gunners. They lost nine B-25s and nine P-38s . Japanese claims were even more outlandish - they claimed 119 victories and lost eighteen fighters.

November 6, 1943: Kawato claimed one B-24 while attacking a formation of sixteen Liberators attempting to bomb a Japanese convoy heading toward Kavieng. One Fifth Air Force B-24 was lost over the Southwest Pacific on this date, but the circumstances are unknown. Although Kawato writes in the forward to his memoir, "I never aimed especially at the cockpit to destroy the pilot of the craft," he contradicts himself by writing that in trying to shoot down this B-24, "I attacked him from the front and above, aiming at the cockpit."

Between November 6 and 10 Kawato claims two TBF Avengers. A check of TBF losses for this period indicates that none were lost.

On November 11th, the U.S. Navy, in conjunction with Fifth Air Force, launched another massive raid against Rabaul. Twenty-three B-24 heavies took off from New Guinea at 0700 to bomb Rabaul's Lakunai Airfield. Carrier Task Groups 50.3 and 50.4 (**Essex, Bunker Hill, Independence, Saratoga,** and **Princeton**) launched their planes at 0645. The 125 carrier based bombers, SBDs, TBFs, and SB2Cs, were escorted by 127 F6F Hellcats. Their target was shipping in Rabaul's Simpson Harbor.

According to Kawato's book - and his POW interrogation statements - he did see action that day. Although he states that he was one of about 120 Zero pilots opposing the enemy, there were in fact, only sixty-eight. He estimates enemy strength at around 700 planes - 100 each of F4Us, P-38s, and P-39s and 200 each of B-24s and TBFs. Kawato claims a P-38 shot down that morning, but there were no P-38s involved. He also recalls that Zeros releasing aerial burst bombs brought down some fifty B-25s. "It was a spectacular sight seeing gasoline on the sea continue to burn well past noon, " he writes. But there were no B-25s on this strike either.

Piloting a TBF that day was Lieutenant William F. "Red" Krantz of VT-17 from the **Bunker Hill**, which launched twenty-six Hellcats and twenty-three SB2Cs in addition to the Avenger squadron. As the strike force approached Rabaul through the St. George Channel, Krantz saw fighters taking off from a dirt strip, kicking up dust.

"We encountered numerous thunderheads at 12,000 feet. Some enemy cruisers, light and small, were dodging in and out of the shadows," recalls Krantz. "At this time, the dive bombers reported aerial burst bombs, along with numerous Zeros who were looking at their first action against the new SB2C. At 0900, Commander Bagdonovich, the Air Group skipper, ordered the dive bombers to attack the cruisers, followed by torpedo planes."

As the torpedo planes were making their runs on the cruisers, Kawato claims that he quit chasing a Corsair to thwart the Avengers. After flaming one TBF, he states that he was shot down by a pair of Corsairs, but managed to bail out at 500 feet. Although there were no Corsairs involved that day, Kawato insists that he was strafed by one of the two that had nailed him. According to his POW interrogation report, this was the first time he had been shot down. It states: "Shot down over Simpson Harbor. Parachuted to sea and swam ashore."

With two Zeros in hot pursuit Krantz made a steep approach to attack a heavy cruiser. He released his torpedo and made a left turn, but was enveloped in a hail of intense anti-aircraft fire from a cruiser and a destroyer. "One AA burst almost blew me upside down. As I passed near the destroyer a heavy plume of smoke poured out of the right side of my engine. I next fired my machine guns at a small enemy ship and headed for St. George Channel."

Krantz's TBF was immediately attacked by two fighters. "I dropped to the top of the waves to prevent them from flying underneath me. My gunner, V.S. Case, accounted for two and an F6F picked off another."

The burning Avenger headed for Empress Augusta Bay on Bougainville Island. However, luck ran out and Krantz was forced to ditch within sight of Buka Island. The three man crew drifted for twelve miserable days in a life

Lieutenant William "Red" Krantz of VT-17, flanked by crewmen O.L. Miller (left) and V.J. Case (right) in front of their Grumman Avenger.

raft before landing at Cape Orford on New Britain Island. After some very close calls with the enemy they were finally rescued on March 26, 1944.

"Red" Krantz (Captain, USN, Ret.) comments on Kawato's account of the November 11th action: "In reading Kawato's book dealing with the November 11th raid, his imagination ran away from him. No B-25s, no F4Us, no P-39s, no P-38s, no 700 aircraft on that raid. He was right about the use of aerial burst bombs that day. Also, our attack was terminated by 9:30 AM, but his remark about gasoline from downed aircraft burning in the sea well past noon is baloney."

American carrier planes claimed thirty-eight victories, ten probables and five damaged over Rabaul that morning. Later that afternoon, while defending their carriers against Japanese bombers escorted by fighters, the navy pilots chalked up another ninety-nine victories and nine damaged. The enemy planes in this latter action were evidently mostly carrier aircraft from the **Shokaku** and **Zuikaku**. The Japanese claimed that their Rabaul-based fighters shot down seventy-one American aircraft that day for the loss of only eleven of their own. Total American Navy losses were six TBFs and eight Grumman Hellcats.

Major Gregory "Pappy" Boyington, CO of VMF-214.

An explanation is in order concerning aerial combat claims. Claims in official records are simply that - claims. When the smoke has cleared and inventory taken, one will invariably find that actual losses were far less than claimed.

American fighter pilots had an incentive to have their victories verified (by gun camera or eye-witnesses) - they joined the fraternity of "aces" by shooting down five or more enemy aircraft. But the Japanese had no such objective and motives. They did not utilize gun cameras in aerial combat; their claims were taken at face value. there were no promotions, medals or publicity; the Japanese did not have "aces".

Kawato claims a P-38 on December 15, 1943 while recovering from wounds suffered on the November 11th raid. He writes that he was severely scolded by the Air Group commander for disobeying orders by flying that day. This is difficult to believe. An enlisted pilot (especially one of Kawato's extreme youth and low rank) simply did not disobey an air group commander in the Japanese Navy . Incidentally, there were no P-38s lost that day.

Kawato reportedly collided with a P-39 about this time. In his interrogation report he gives the date as December 15, 1943; in his memoir it was Christmas Day.

In fact, the short ranged P-39s were never sent over Rabaul. On December 17, 1943, Major "Pappy" Boyington led thirty-one F4Us, twenty-two F6Fs, and twenty-three New Zealand P-40 Kittyhawks to Rabaul - the first time ever for single-engined, land-based fighters. Two Zeros were claimed by a Hellcat and a Corsair and there were no American losses. The New Zealanders claimed five victories and lost two aircraft. The Japanese suffered only one loss that day.

Kawato's victim was not a P-39, but a P-40 flown by Flight Lieutenant John O. McFarlane. He was last seen diving vertically after he was hit. His aircraft disappeared behind Mt. Turanguna into the bay north of that hill. Kawato and McFarlane landed in the water not from each other, and both were individually retrieved by Japanese rescue boats. McFarlane was taken prisoner and was never heard from again.

Around December 20, 1943 Kawato claimed an F4U Corsair but fails to elaborate. In checking with the mission logs of his unit, we find that Kawato did fly on the 20th; twenty-seven Zeros went up but encountered no enemy aircraft. Kawato did not fly again until the 27th when thirty-two Zeros claimed six Republic P-43s * and two F4Fs. There were no claims for F4Us.

However, it was Kawato's claim to have bested the legendary Pappy Boyington that has given him some celebrity status. Indeed, the twenty-eight victory ace was shot down on January 3, 1944 near New Ireland Island.

*The Japanese had met a few of this type in China and a handful in their attacks on the Philippine Air Force in '41-'42, but none served thereafter with U.S. forces.

A pair of Chance Vought F4U-1A Corsairs of VMF-214. Boyington was not flying his personal aircraft, #86, on the day he was shot down, a fact overlooked by Kawato. (Depiction by Shori Tanaka)

The War History Office of the Japan Defense Agency has provided proof that Kawato flew on January 3rd. Thirty-seven Zeros of the 253rd Kokutai led by Lieutenant Kenji Nakagawa scrambled and engaged an estimated thirty F4U Corsairs from 0615 to 0650. The American time observed was about an hour later, 0715 to 0750. The 204th Kokutai also joined the battle with thirty-three Zeros. The 253rd claimed five destroyed and two probables (all F4Us), while the 204th claimed three Corsairs destroyed, one probable and one Hellcat kill. Two F4Us were actually lost - those flown by Boyington and his wingman, Captain George Ashmun and no Hellcats were lost.

According to the 253rd's mission log, Kawato flew in the second squadron of twenty-two Zeros. He was flying in the number three position of a four plane flight, led by Petty Officer Takamori Yamanaka (#1) and including Petty Officers Kesajiro Nakaya (#2) and Masayuki Osada (#4).

According to Dr. Masamichi Inoki, L.L.D., former President of the Japan National Defense Agency, and his assistant, Mr. Masahiro Yoshimatsu, chief researcher for the agency's WW II Research Section: "Kawato, Masajiro piloted the third aircraft in a formation of four and his assigned duty was to fly protective cover for the Japanese fighters actually engaged in the aerial combat in which Major G. Boyington was downed. Kawato Masajiro had a reputation among his fellow pilots as having plenty of guts. His courage in combat is not in question, but in so far as the battle of January 3, 1944 is concerned, his claim for credit is groundless and without a basis in fact."

Strangely, Kawato writes in his book that his downing of Boyington "was the thirteenth kill credited to me." In June of 1943 the Imperial Navy High Command issued a directive discontinuing the practice of recording individual aerial victories. All victories claimed were to be credited to the unit. The flight record of the 253 Kokutai for January 3rd shows no individual credits.

In any "who shot down whom" match up, the details must coincide with those recorded by the opposition. Kawato's own recollections of this particular combat simply doesn't meet the necessary criteria. It isn't enough to say, "I shot down Pappy Boyington."

Kawato claims that he spotted Boyington's fighter over Duke of York Island as it was being pursued by other Zeros. He writes: "I kept my cool and waited until I had the right distance. After fifteen or sixteen rounds of 20 mm gunfire, some hitting the cabin near the cockpit, it started to smoke a little, but no flames. He rolled over to the right and went in for a dive, but I was able to stay with him because of my speed...As he was going on over Rabaul, where our base was located, I was thinking how far this Corsair (F4U) would be able to escape me."

In a 1984 telephone interview, Boyington had this to say about Kawato's claim: "I was never anywhere near Duke of York Island or Rabaul on the day I was shot down. To begin with, we used the term 'Rabaul' to mean the Rabaul area, not necessarily the town of Rabaul nor the harbor. Kawato took the term literally from my book."

Colonel Boyington continues: "I ended up in the water almost abreast of Cape St. George, New Ireland, about five miles from shore. I knew we had a coast watcher at this point and had high hopes of having him rescue me. The main reason the fight took place fifty miles away from their base is elementary - they picked us up on radar and were coming out to intercept us. The Japanese had no way of knowing that we were fighters, not bombers."

There are two illustrations in Kawato's book, as well as several paintings and prints, showing Kawato's Zero shooting down Boyington's Corsair (#86). Although #86 was Boyington's personal mount, he was not flying it on the day he was shot down. Boyington further adds: "As for the plane I was flying, I had taken Marion Carl's plane at Vella La Vella, our home base, on the afternoon of January 2. I led the fighters that were to go on that early morning mission to the Rabaul area, to Bougainville where we stayed the night. My original plane that I referred to was actually the plane I had borrowed from Marion Carl the day before."

Pappy Boyington and George Ashmun were shot down by a group of Zero pilots whose identities will never be known. It is not certain which units were involved - the 204th or the 253rd. It has been printed elsewhere that Warrant Officer Takeo Tanimizu (now of Osaka, Japan) may have been one of the pilots who actually shot down Boyington. However, Mr. Tanimizu has made it very clear that he cannot recall the precise details of this combat simply because there were so many combats and time has faded his memory. Boyington survived the downing and Japanese prison damp.

Boyington later claimed three victories and his wingman, George Ashmun, received credit for one. Other land based Navy and Marine Corps fighters claimed five more victories and five probables. The 253rd Kokutai suffered just one Zero damaged (1st Squadron) while the 204th lost two planes and pilots: Petty Officers Hideshi Tanimoto and Yoshige Kitade.

How did Kawato's "I shot down Pappy Boyington" myth originate? It started in 1976 when the two pilots were brought together for a publicity interview. This was during the time that Boyington was working as a technical advisor for the TV series, Baa Baa Blacksheep (later changed to Blacksheep Squadron). In their first meeting, conversing through an interpreter, "Mike" Kawato was asked if he had ever heard of Pappy Boyington or the Blacksheep Squadron. Kawato had professed that he did not. Nevertheless, the two old pilots had a great time together and Boyington later gave his new friend a signed copy of his book.

"After a few episodes of the TV show aired, I got a call from Kawato," recalled Boyington. He told me that he had just finished reading my book and said he was very sorry to say this, but believed he was the pilot who shot me down. He was very apologetic about it." Boyington at first took Kawato's word for it, but later, when he started checking out the details given by Kawato, he came to the conclusion that "this wasn't the guy who got me."

Kawato stretched his credibility even further by telling a **Wisconsin State Journal** newspaper reporter (Oshkosh Air Show, August 7, 1983) that "he knew Boyington's plane by its markings and that his squadron leader backs his claim." This was a ludicrous statement. Lieutenant Kenji Nakagawa, who led the Zeros that day, was killed on November 3, 1944 over Leyte Gulf in the Philippines. Kawato's company commander, Warrant Officer Shigeo Fukumoto died in a car accident in 1945. As for the fate of his flight members, Takamori Yamanaka survived the war but died of illness on March 21, 1955; Masayuki Osada was killed in action on January 6, 1944, followed by Kesajiro Nakaya eight days later.

Kawato in Zero pilot's garb, poses with a flying Zero at Ed Maloney's Plane of Fame Air Museum at Chino Airport, California in 1988.

Pappy Boyington passed away on January 11,1988 at the age of seventy-five. He died of cancer in Fresno, California where he made his home. A Medal of Honor winner, he was a popular figure at air shows. For several years prior to his passing, Kawato and Boyington would trade barbs at air shows while the media and the public took in the "combat" between two former pilots. Boyington said he took delight in verbally "shooting down Kawato".

On February 6, 1944 Kawato claimed a P-38 over Rabaul and supposedly rammed a B-24 and parachuted into the sea off Cape St. George. Although nineteen Liberators of the 5th Bomb Group did attack Rabaul that day, there was no fighter opposition and all returned safely. There were also no P-38s on this mission. In his POW interrogation report, Kawato makes no mention of the ramming incident and simply stated: "Shot down over Simpson Harbor, parachuted into the sea and swam ashore."

Suffering from a leg injury, Kawato was left behind with a handful of other pilots after the main force of the 253rd pulled back to Truk on February 20, 1944.

The rear guard force of the detached 253rd was slowly reorganized into a fighting unit. Mechanics and engineers labored day and night to repair about a dozen junk Zero fighters; they also remanufactured two new ones from wrecks.

Kawato participated in two dogfights with Marine F4Us on March 3rd and 12th, 1944 over Tobera Airfield. Although the Japanese made a number of claims no Corsairs were lost. On March 22nd he and three other pilots shot down a Marine PBJ over Simpson Harbor. From then on he flew reconnaissance missions to the Admiralties until November 1944.

The existence of official American and Allied military records and a limited amount of Japanese records have proven to be a bane for Kawato. Unaware that his claims could be checked, Kawato writes of his scouting mission to the Admiralties on September 15, 1944. It was an uneventful reconnaissance mission to the Admiralties. However, he takes some liberties stating that while being chased by enemy fighters, he decided to strafe the enemy airfield on Emirau Island.

"In order to avoid detection I went down as low as possible near the surface of the ocean skimming about twenty feet above wave tops," Kawato writes. "After I made the turn from north to east, I turned my gun switch to 'ON' and went over a small hill. I saw an airfield. There were approximately fifty medium size and small craft on the field. I swooped down on them pulling the trigger tightly. I caught them 'with their pants down'." He claims to have set fire to about ten planes.

Robert Millington, formerly with Marine PBJ squadron VMB-413 writes: "Please note my comments ... regarding his alleged September 15th attack on Emirau. I was at Munda at the time. I didn't arrive at Emirau until October 18, 1944. I never heard a word about this alleged raid. MAG-61 with VMB-433 and VMB-443 had been at Emirau since mid-July 1944, along with VMB-611 which joined them later. VMD-254 was also attached. Never a word was ever mentioned of such an attack. If it had happened, I surely would have heard something about it during the five months I was there. Lieutenant Colonel Stewart Ralston was Operation Officer of MAG-61 and although he was not there on September 15th, as he came to Munda in early September to take command of VMB-413, when we got back to Emirau in October, he was again Group Operations Officer, and he told me that he never heard of such an attack."

The War Diary of MAG-61 for September 15, 1944 states: "The first anniversary of VMB-433 and 443 was celebrated by both squadrons. All operations were secured for the day and a sports program was carried out by the squadron's enlisted personnel while the officers held a party at the Officer's Club. Captain Phelps of 254 flew daily photo coverage of the Kavieng and Panapai airdromes."

Uneventful reconnaissance missions were the norm during the summer and fall of 1944. But on November 9, 1944 three Zeros were fitted with bombs and sent out to attack an enemy airfield on Los Negros Island (Admiralties). They were detected by radar eighty miles out, but misidentified as "friendlies". Kawato piloted the lead aircraft, carrying Ensign Chuhei Okubo (mission leader) in the rear of his double-seat Zero. The bombing attack did very little damage and all three aircraft returned safely.

On March 9, 1945 Kawato and Petty Officer Second Class Tokio Shimizu (observer) took off in a two-seat Zero to attack enemy ground forces in the Wide Bay area. Near the vicinity of Cape Orford, he spotted an Australian gunboat (ML-825) and attacked it. He missed with two bombs, came back on a strafing run and was hit. He ditched his plane about a mile away, but his back seat observer was killed.

Kawato writes: "As I was making a wide turn, I spotted a small destroyer going at full speed under the clouds...My first bomb hit midstern and I counted only ten shots out of seventy as effective. The destroyer stopped suddenly and smoke burst out of two or three places. I must have hit a vital spot. I turned over at 4,500 feet and went into a second attack. I dropped my second bomb at the height of 900 feet and hit "Bull's Eye'."

And the fiction continues. "...I had made up my mind to dive into the destroyer as soon as possible." He claims to have plowed his burning Zero into the sea - only to wake up two days later floating in his life jacket.

Greg Boyington (left) enjoys a chat with former Zero pilot Masahiro Mitsuda in 1988.

"I couldn't move my right leg," he writes. "I felt my thigh. It was torn up and flabby and burned with pain when I touched it. I moved my body to check for further injuries. My back hurt and I was wounded on my right side. My left wrist hurt too. Furthermore, my left arm was numb. Shaking, I touched my left shoulder and found that it was dislocated. My left arm was swollen to the size of my thigh and turning purple. I even had a wound on my left thigh and a gash on my head.

Not wanting to be captured Kawato writes that he attempted suicide by shooting himself in the head with his pistol. In 1980 he described his weapon as a "small German automatic about .22 or .25 caliber." By 1991 this gun had grown. In the December 12, 1991 edition of the **Journal American** (a Washington state newspaper), Kawato stated: "It was an American Colt automatic." The Colt Auto, standard sidearm of the American military in WW II is a .45 caliber "hand cannon" and quite fatal when fired against one's temple.

Whatever version the reader chooses to believe, Kawato writes that his gun failed to fire: "The pistol wasn't loaded, but I managed to cock it by clasping the gun between my teeth...Click! A dud! In a dazed state I reloaded the gun in the same manner and pulled the trigger again. Blaaak! The noise was loud enough to split my eardrum and I drifted off into black nothingness."

The following statement from Kawato's POW medical report at the time of his capture illustrates the scope of his literary license: "Fractured left wrist, multiple healed small gunshot wounds. Surgeon considers treatment of wrist may be safely left until arrival at First Aust. Army."

"I spent over two months surviving in the jungle," stated Kawato in 1980. "I crawled around looking for food and survived off the land. I tied my swollen leg with potato vine. Life was very difficult in the jungle."

According to Australian records he was "Captured 14 March 1945 by ANGAU (Australia New Guinea

Administrative Unit), after being ashore nearly five days with nothing to eat."

It is noted that Kawato was well treated as a prisoner. In return he divulged important military information about the strength and weaknesses of his unit, locations of fuel dumps, underground shelters, airfield installations, headquarters, and gun emplacements. The existence of his prisoner interrogation report must have been shocking to Kawato who had no idea that such a document ever existed. It has now come back to haunt him.

Major R.E.M. Cameron, who interrogated Kawato, wrote the following assessment: "Nineteen years of age, eight years education, three years military service. Intelligent, normally observant and answered all questions freely. He was arrogant and proud to be a pilot. Fellow POWs in hospital consider him mentally unstable...information obtained is considered reliable as parts which could be checked are consistent with known facts."

Long after the war a copy of Kawato's interrogation report was forwarded to Commander Tomoyoshi Hori, his former squadron executive officer now aged eighty-four. Commander Hori reviewed the four page report and concluded that his subordinate's statements were generally correct.

During Kawato's interrogation he stated that he was shot down three times, parachuted three times, and collided once. It is interesting to note that, while boastful by nature, he made no claims for intentionally ramming enemy aircraft. Forty years later, he would claim that he had been shot down twice, parachuted four times, and rammed enemy aircraft three times.

In his memoir Kawato stated that he flew a total of over 1,200 hours in WW II - about 900 in combat. This total contradicts the figure of 200 combat hours which he gave his interrogators. According to unit records Kawato flew thirty-five combat missions from December 1, 1943 until February 6, 1944. His last dogfight occurred on March 12, 1944. After this date, he flew sporadic reconnaissance missions to the Admiralties.

"I shot down nineteen planes during the war." Kawato proclaims today.

His interrogation report says: "He claims 18 kills in 200 hours combat including a B-24. Most of his kills were 'Sikorskys'(F4Us) from Green Island."

Could he really have shot down that many enemy aircraft, considering his limited combat experience? It must also be remembered that the Zero fighter was badly outclassed by Hellcats and Corsairs.

This question was put to Takeo Tanimizu and Sadamu Komachi, both of whom served in Kawato's squadron. Said Tanimizu: "How can a novice pilot like Kawato, with less than 200 combat hours possibly shoot down eighteen American planes? His kill claim is just absurd."

Komachi was just as adamant: "His kill claim is utter nonsense."

Both of these pilots were hard core veterans, highly regarded in the small circle of surviving Zero fighter pilots.

Kawato's aerial victory total which could be documented, amounts to 1.25 (RNZAF P-40 with which he collided, and one quarter credit shared with three other pilots in the destruction of a PBJ.)

It is certain that Kawato exaggerated his combat claims in order to impress his interrogator. He had good reason to try and impress others. As a baby-faced eighteen year old novice from Japan, he was ridiculed on at least one occasion by officers at Rabaul. One of them pointed to Kawato during a squadron lineup (in the presence of the air group commander) and said aloud, "We wonder if a child like you can actually fight in this war." This statement came from Kawato's own book and one by Dr. Yasuho Izawa.

This remark infuriated Kawato, filling him with an understandable anger - and a burning desire to prove himself at any cost.

On July 31, 1945 Masajiro Kawato was transferred to the custody of the U.S. Army Provost Marshal Department in Manila for further interrogation. From the Phillipines he returned seemingly from the dead, to Japan later that year.

Masajiro Kawato had a distinguished career as a Zero fighter pilot and was highly regarded by troops at Rabaul. His true combat exploits were far more interesting than the myths found in his memoir.

Kawato now lives in Redmond, Washington and spends a great deal of his time selling his memoirs, attending air and militaria shows, signing autographs and giving lectures on World War II.

"Mike" Kawato at the Great Western Militaria Show, Pomona, CA, in November 1992.

THE RESCUE OF ED MIKES

Five hundred and four American and Allied aviators owe their lives to the U.S. Submarine Service of WWII. They were rescued from enemy waters in some of the most daring and dangerous operations of the war. The most documented rescue involved P-51 pilot, Captain Edward Mikes Jr. The teamwork of U.S. Navy and Army Air Force units to rescue this lone American was nothing short of heroic.

On August 3, 1945 - less than two weeks before the end of the war - the Seventh Fighter Command sent the 506th Fighter Group to brutalize Tokyo area targets. Sixty P-51s, twenty each from the 457th, 458th, and the 462nd Fighter Squadrons, took off from their base on Iwo Jima. Led by Lieutenant Colonel Harley Brown, their mission was to strafe targets of opportunity, particularly airfields, railway installations and trains.

Captain Edward Mikes Jr. of the 458th, leading Green Flight, arrived over Chofu Airfield west of Tokyo, home base for the Japanese Army's 52nd Sentai (air group). What remaining fighters (Franks and Oscars) they had were carefully hidden, so Mikes decided to follow some railroad tracks to see what they might produce. "While following the rails, I noticed a Jap armored tank moving the same direction we were," recalls Mikes. "I lined the tank up in my sights and gave it a good long burst. I saw many strikes on it. Then I zoomed on course. The tank was located slightly west of Atsugi and just after passing it, my airplane started running rough." The Mustang had fallen victim to ground fire. The time was 1145.

"I checked all my instruments and found I had no oil pressure," Mikes continues. "I told my flight I was hit and directed them to take me to the Rally Point. Just after we passed the shoreline, my engine started to give off

The center of attention on August 3, 1945: Capt.Edward Mikes Jr. of the 458th Ftr Sq, shown here as an instructor in Florida. (Ed Mikes)

white smoke and I started losing airspeed. I knew I was going to have to bail out soon so I loosened my safety belt and shoulder straps. My airspeed was down to 150 mph. I rolled the canopy back and then jettisoned it and told my flight I was hitting the silk. I started out, but my plane

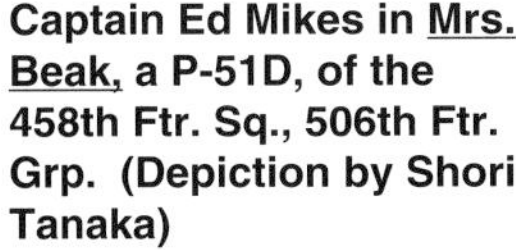

Captain Ed Mikes in <u>Mrs. Beak,</u> a P-51D, of the 458th Ftr. Sq., 506th Ftr. Grp. (Depiction by Shori Tanaka)

started to stall and go into a spin. I climbed back in and got out of the spin at 2,500 feet. I put my flaps down and started to climb out again, but my right foot got stuck and I had to give an extra shove, and finally I was free."

Nothing ever goes according to plan. Captain Mikes was slammed into the rudder. He thought he was going to pass out. His descent into the bay was hardly serene, "I pulled my ripcord and got an awful jolt. My left arm went limp and I thought it was broken. It came back to life gradually. On the way down I tried to release my chute but it wouldn't release by just hitting the quick release. I hit the water and then used two hands to release the chute and in the meantime my feet were getting tangled in the shroud lines. I got the chute pack off and inflated my life vest. I then proceeded to inflate my dinghy." Mikes lit a smoke flare to let his comrades know that he was OK.

Bulgin' Bessie a B-17G of the USAAF 4 Emergency Rescue Squadron, Iwo Jima 1945. (Marian R. Shaw)

Captain Nolen Johnson of Blue Flight called for **Jukebox 70** (an Air-Sea Rescue B-17G of the 4th Emergency Rescue Squadron). At 1155, Staff Sergeant Laverle H. Westerman (radioman) heard the call, "Splash in the Bay." (See map, page 93.)

The dory hung bomber, piloted by Second Lieutenant Burt Klatt and carrying a crew of nine, headed for the bailout. First Lieutenant Vaughn E. Sowers from Ed Mikes' flight raced in to meet BULGIN'BESSIE at the entrance to the bay. It was a mistake. The top turret gunner let loose with his .50s at the fast approaching unidentified aircraft. Sowers withdrew and approached more cautiously. There was no problem the second time.

Now the Japanese started getting into the act. A picket boat was dispatched from Misaki. The stranded pilot was only four miles offshore. Lieutenant Sowers nipped that in the bud. He strafed and sank it. On the horizon Mikes was elated to see a B-17 and a B-29 approaching him. The Superfortress had also heard the distress call and joined in. The two lumbering bombers began circling Mikes like giant vultures. His descent into the bay and the ongoing rescue attempt could hardly be ignored by the enemy on shore. The drama was being watched with keen interest by telescope. The Yokosuka Naval Defense Command placed an urgent call to the Navy's 302nd Kokutai at Atsugi. "Get some aircraft airborne," came the order.

Lieutenant Yutaka Morioka, Zero squadron leader of the 302nd Kokutai at Atsugi. He lost his left hand to a B-29, but returned to combat with an iron claw. (Y. Morioka)

Lieutenant Yutaka Morioka, the twenty-three year old squadron leader of Zeros, got his scramble orders. He had four aircraft brought up from the underground shelter and readied for combat. His flight consisted of Lieutenant Ohta, Lieutenant (jg) Ono, and Petty Officer Yoshi Yokozuka. Morioka, a naval academy graduate, had originally been a Val dive bomber pilot but converted to Zeros in 1944. On January 23,1945 he lost his left hand to the tail stinger of a B-29 near Nagoya. Within a few months, he returned to combat with a hook in place of his missing hand.

First Lieutenant Cliff Shaw, navigator aboard the circling B-17, was working frantically to prepare starting instructions for the motorized wooden Higgins boat. The one ton, twenty-seven foot boat was designed to carry three times its weight in men and equipment. It was powered by a twin five horsepower engine (top speed was eight mph) with sufficient fuel capacity for 400 miles. It was crammed with the latest survival gear and creature comforts. It was a sportsman's dream.

Shaw recalls, "A few days before Wunderling's crew dropped a boat to a pilot down in the bay and fought off a Japanese patrol boat but the pilot made no effort to start the engines and move out to the sub. He was never heard from - so I wasn't about to drop our boat until our instructions were aboard."

At 1216 the Super Dumbo arrived over Mikes. He had marked his position with dye marker and orange smoke flares. Shaw completed his note with these final items: "1. Drop chutes. 2. Start engines. 3. Steer 133 degrees to sub. God be with you."

"Go around!" yelled Cliff Shaw to the pilot. It was 1223. Mikes was incredulous as the bomber passed right over him. It was a perfect run. "Why hadn't they dropped the boat?" he wondered.

Tech sergeant Ollie West, the engineer, was having trouble reaching through the special opening in the bomb bay door to place the map in the instructions compartment of the lifeboat. The B-17 turned into the wind for a second run in grand view of the great Tokyo plains and majestic Mount Fuji to the west. It was now 1228 and Ollie was still having trouble. "No good, go around again," snapped Shaw to the pilot. Burt Klatt was agitated.

"By this time Burt was ready to drop, using his own drop switch," recalls Shaw. "We were vulnerable with no chin turret, no belly turret and no one manning the top turret." Zeros were reported lurking in the area.

At 1230 BULGIN' BESSIE turned into the wind for the third run. Ollie had finished his task. At 1233 it was "Boat away!" They circled back and saw the boat land about thirty yards from the downed flier. Satisfied that their job was done, it was now time for Super Dumbo to get out.

Mikes paddled to the boat and climbed in. He released the chutes, put the rudder in place, and proceeded to start the motor. It took six pulls to engage the engine. Poor Cliff Shaw - Ed Mikes was in such haste he hadn't even bothered to read his instructions.

Meanwhile the submarine **Aspro** (SS-309), on its seventh war patrol, received word from the Super Dumbo that a wooden boat had been dropped to a downed pilot in Sagami Nada. The position given put the survivor further into the bay than first reported and that was risky. Commander James H. Ashley, Jr. ordered full speed ahead. Ashley took charge of the rescue operation and communicated instructions to the aircraft via VHF. He had a loyal crew that would have followed him anywhere and nothing gave them more satisfaction than rescuing a "zoomie" (downed pilot). (See map, page 90.)

Two Navy four-engined Privateers (PB4Y-2s) of VPB-121 (Fleet Air Wing 18) took up the guardianship of Ed Mikes about five minutes after the B-17 departed. They had been ship hunting along the coast. Lieutenant Commander Raymond J. Pflum in LOTTA TAYLE, and his wingman, Lieutenant Ralph D. Ettinger, piloting DANGEROUS DAN, offered their services to the **Aspro**. Enroute to the submarine, the Privateers had spotted a Japanese transport ship. After missing with bombs on the first pass, Pflum scored a direct hit on the second and the transport sank within forty seconds.

A Higgins boat is strapped under the belly of a B-17. (NASM/ Smithsonian 82-8322)

"Boat away!" The Higgins is dropped. (NASM/ Smithsonian 82-8321)

A Higgins boat, shown here in demonstration, was extraordinarily seaworthy and could take considerable punishment, as Mikes proved. (NASM/Smithsonian 82-8319)

Thirty-five year old Ray Pflum from Chicago was an old China Clipper pilot. He was absolutely fearless and sometimes took unnecessary risks, but he produced results. When it came to bombing, he was a pro; he held the distinction of having dropped a record 112,500 pounds of bombs on Wake Island. Sometimes when the hunting was good, he and his crew were sinking eight to ten ships a day. Ed Mikes couldn't have had a better guardian angel.

Major Malcolm C. Watters was overhead with his 506th Fighter Group Mustangs. It being his thirteenth mission he had decided to lead the sub cover flight. He recalls:

"The four of us were called to provide cover for **Aspro**. After circling the sub at about 1,500 feet, we were jumped by twelve or fourteen Zeros coming out of the sun. We were circling in elements into each other per standard procedure when I saw bullets hitting the wing of my element leader. I immediately released my wing tanks (about 150 gallons) and tried to turn into the Zeros. The right tank came off - the left tank stayed on. Lieutenant Coneff passed by me pulling vapor trails off his wing tips. I told him to relax on the controls. I thought he was in a high speed stall the last time I saw him as he approached the ocean. He did a full roll and went in upside down."

Morioka comments on his encounter with Lieutenant Coneff. "I and three other pilots flew to Atami (a city on the shore of Tokyo Bay) and I found there in the bright sunshine, a lifeboat and an approaching submarine. Above them were two B-24s and higher still, four P-51s guarding. We approached the P-51s from the rear and higher. The P-51s did not spot us nor did the submarine open fire. From a distance of about 500 meters I fired my 13mm guns at the P-51 at the extreme left of the formation to find the range, then at about 100 meters, I fired my 20 mm cannons, hitting the aircraft. Fearing a collision, I zoomed up. Looking down, I saw three P-51s and a big white circle on the sea."

Second Lieutenant John J. Coneff of the 457th, fatally hit, had plunged into the water from 3,500 feet. The Zeros and Mustangs played tag but the Americans were low on fuel and could not afford to dogfight. It was 625 miles back to Iwo.

Lt. Yutaka Morioka in the cockpit of his A6M5 Model 52 Zero. He is gripping the throttle with his iron claw. (Yutaka Morioka)

Morioka pursued one aircraft on the deck, but the Mustang pilot simply opened full throttle and left him eating his exhaust. "I gave up on the pursuit as too far from the mainland. There would be other P-51s," declared Morioka. "I saw my men dogfighting but the Mustangs flew south. I could see B-24s in the distance but thought the Mustangs would recover and come back, so we retreated from our inferior, low position." The four Zeros assembled and headed for home. Along the way they spotted the wake of a small boat steering its way out of the bay. Morioka nosed his plane down and his three wingmen followed.

Captain Mikes hunkered down in the boat. What he had first thought were four Mustangs covering the submarine's approach soon exhibited hostile intent. "I immediately fell to the bottom of the boat and hugged the right side," he recalls, "as much out of sight as possible and I kept my left arm on the rudder trying to keep my craft on the same heading." Mikes felt certain he would never survive the strafing. He was going to be so much hamburger.

Lieutenant Morioka sighted the wooden boat through his reflector gunsight and started firing. He was followed in turn by each of his three wingmen. A line of splintering punctures ripped through the center of the boat like a giant buzzsaw. Mikes was grazed in the left wrist and needled with splinters.

But the wooden vessel refused to sink, thanks to its many watertight compartments. Morioka decided to give it another try and took his wingmen around. The downed flyer survived the first round but he was facing incredible odds. Another deadly hail of 13mm rounds chewed into the boat. The rubber life raft alongside the boat was like a sieve. "While we were strafing the boat," recalls Morioka, "I thought I saw a black shadow jump into the sea."

Each plane had expended over 1,000 rounds in their unfriendly act, yet the "Flying Dutchman" was still defiantly afloat. The sea rescue unit of the AAF Material Command's equipment laboratory, which designed the boat, would have been proud. Their product had passed the most rigid field test imaginable.

Fortunately for Mikes, the Navy Privateers came to his defense and the Zeros quickly departed. Mikes made a circular motion with his arms to let them know he wanted them to circle him. In the distance he could see **Aspro** with men on deck and steered his boat towards her.

But there was yet more trouble on the horizon. The Privateer crews had seen seaplanes gaining altitude over Tateyama (the aircraft belonged to the Tateyama Kokutai). Mikes was within fifty feet of the **Aspro** when he saw an unwelcome party crasher. "I was so close I could feel the heat puffs from the engine exhaust ports," lamented Mikes. The enemy seaplane (codenamed Pete) was starting its glide bombing attack on the **Aspro**.

USS Aspro (US Naval Institute)

"As we were practically dead in the water, we could only flood down and hope for the best," reported Commander Ashley. The **Aspro** lobbed a few rounds of 20mm at the Pete before crash diving, scoring hits in the left wing. The Privateers turned toward the attacker, but the Pete managed to drop two bombs. **Aspro** reached a depth of twenty-five feet when the bombs detonated about 100 feet away.

Flying their four engined giants like fighters, Pflum and Ettinger charged head-on into the intruder. Their gunners were knocking pieces off the biplane as both turned and locked onto the fleeing enemy. Pflum was right on the Pete's tail. John C. Sellman, the plane captain, got a sobering view of the kill. "We were chasing the Pete at a very low altitude, 200-300 feet. As the bow guns and the top turret guns fired on the Pete, you could see the plane going to pieces. The pilot of the Pete did stand up in the cockpit as if he were going to jump. If he parachuted at this low altitude, he had no chance."

Looking through the periscope, Ashley saw the seaplane crash into the sea about a mile away. Ed Mikes had the best seat in the house but wasn't enjoying the drama playing out around him.

A close call! A bomb from a Pete seaplane detonates on the water near the submerged Aspro. Close proximity to the coast of Honshu is apparent in this photo taken from a Privateer.

Tateyama Kokutai Pete, TA-3, going down in flames. This is an actual photo taken from one of the two PB4Ys on August 3, 1945.

The crew of Lotta Tayle enjoy a pre-flight smoke. Front row (l. to r.): ARM2/c Tommy Winters, Lt.(jg) F.J. Meinhardt, Lt.(jg) W.T. Hough, Lt. Cmdr. Raymond J. Pflum, Lt. Carson (not on Mikes mission), AMM 1/c John C. Sellman. Standing (l. to r.): AOM3/c A.H. Wampler, AOM 1/c R.A. Lenegan, ARM 1/c G.W. Emerson, AOM Robert Biddle, AMM 2/c A.W. Bowden, AMM 1/c E.J. Bocade. (John C. Sellman)

With the enemy dispatched, Commander Ashley brought **Aspro** topside at 1326. Ed Mikes was coming alongside when another intruder came upon the scene. It was another Pete, in the clear, coming in from a high altitude. "Take her down, " yelled Commander Ashley and **Aspro** crash dived for the second time.

Captain Mikes huddled in his boat. The routine was beginning to get all too familiar. It had all the elements of a hackneyed Hollywood war flick. Never in his life had he been the focus of so much unwanted attention.

The second Pete dropped two bombs that exploded with a terrific concussion about fifty feet in front of the submarine. Once again, the Privateers worked in tandem to knock the intruder from the sky. William J. Satzer, radioman aboard DANGEROUS DAN, had a ringside sea. "It was on our starboard side when we overtook it," he remembers. "Three of our turrets with six .50 caliber machine guns were firing at it. I watched the Pete's rear gunner expecting him to be firing at us but saw no sign of it. (I had some gunnery training with at SBD

Crew of Dangerous Dan. Front Row, (l. to r.): ARM2/c F.H. Long, AOM 3/c D.K. Ledman, AMM3/c P.G. O'Carroll, AOM 1/c L. Morrell, and ARM 3/c Bill Satzer. Standing (l. to r.): AOM 2/c C.H. Davis, AMM 1/c H.H. Lemberger, Lt.(jg) J.C. Mickelsen, Lt. Cmdr. Ralph D. Ettinger, Lt.(jg) Ezekiel H. Daughtrey, ACRM Howard H. Commons, and AMM 2/c R.C. Prior. (Bill Satzer)

Crew of Bulgin' Bessie, Iwo Jima, July 1945. From left: Staff Sgt. Laverle H. Westerman, T/Sgt. Oliver West, 2nd Lt. Burt Klatt, Staff Sgt. David Wren, 1st Lt. Cliff Shaw, and Staff Sgt. Eugene Carson. Back row: Staff Sgt. Frank Winosky and Staff Sgt. Jack Honeycutt. (Laverle Westerman)

Lt. John Clifford Shaw, navigator of the Super Dumbo B-17, Bulgin' Bessie.

Rear Admiral James H. Ashley Jr. As a commander he was skipper of the submarine Aspro.

Well deserved Navy Crosses for PB4Y aircraft commanders, Pflum (center) and Ettinger, from Admiral Murray.

Radioman Bill Satzer in 1945. He and every member of his crew received the Distinguished Flying Cross. (Bill Satzer)

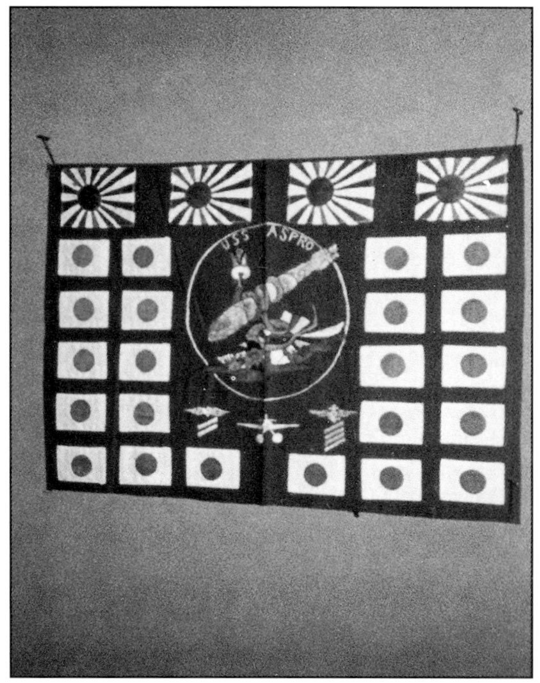

Aspro's victory banner kept by the Aspro veterans. The silhouette of a seaplane denotes the Pete they helped knock down as it attempted to bomb them. The four hash marks under the Gold Wings represent aviators rescued, and the flags denote Japanese ships sunk on two war patrols.

Dauntless operational training unit, and I surely would have been shooting back if I was in the Pete). I expected the Japanese plane to explode in flames, but it pulled up in a steep climbing turn and then dove into the sea. It looked like the pilot had been mortally wounded by our fire and jerked at the plane's controls causing it to crash. There was no sign of survivors."

Who were the crews of the two Petes which had attacked the **Aspro**? Tateyama Kokutai's records have identified them as Chief Petty Officer Giichi Sugiura and Petty Officer First Class Tadashi Suzuki, with Chief Petty Officer Kokichi Nishida and Petty Officer First Class Kenzo Yamagata. None survived their encounters with the Privateers.

"When the sub crash dived again I was ready to cash in my chips," said Mikes. "I felt sure they wouldn't come back and I wouldn't have blamed them"

At 1344 the **Aspro** resurfaced, much to the downed pilot's surprise, and two crewmen jumped into action. "I came alongside, shut the throttle on the boat, jumped on the bow of my boat and grabbed the arms of two men reaching for me," recalls Mikes. "I jumped over the railing and said 'Let's get the Hell out of here.' and I started to run the wrong way. One of the men grabbed me and said, 'That's just the Hell what we are going to do. Here, go this way.' I was down the hatch in no time at all." Ed Mikes was given a shot of "medicinal" alcohol by Chief Pharmacist Mate Waldo Larson to treat his splinter wounds and his injured psyche. He had surely earned it.

On August 20, 1945 Lieutenant Commander Pflum and Lieutenant Ettinger were decorated by Vice Admiral

G.D. Murray with the well deserved Navy Cross. Each member of the crew received the Distinguished Flying Cross.

On December 4, 1991 in the lobby of the Hawaiian Regent Hotel in Honolulu, former Zero pilot Yutaka Morioka was approached by a tall distinguished looking gentleman in a gray suit. "Shibaraku desu ne?" (It's been a long time, hasn't it?), said a grinning Ed Mikes to Morioka in perfect Japanese.

Morioka responded earnestly, "I'm very sorry about our first meeting." They shook hands and embraced each other in the spirit of friendship.

"You are alive today because our shooting was bad," quipped Morioka.

"Yeah, I know, and I'm glad," retorted Mikes. The message was clear: No hard feelings.

This most unusual reunion between Edward Mikes and Yutaka Morioka was orchestrated by aviation writer/publisher Jack Lambert and the Seventh Fighter Command Association. The mini-reunion was part of their bigger reunion, set to coincide with the Fiftieth Anniversary of Pearl Harbor.

At their December 5, 1991 meeting in Hawaii Ed Mikes shows Yutaka Morioka his splinter scar received in Morioka's strafing attack.

Edward Mikes ended his career with the rank of major in the Air Force Reserves and is now retired from his job with International Harvester. He makes his home in Arkansas.

Yutaka Morioka is now a certified public accountant living in Tokyo. Of his three wingmen, Ohta's whereabouts are unknown; Ono died in 1950 and Yoshi Yokozuka is alive and well. Burt Klatt, pilot of BULGIN' BESSIE died in 1990. Cliff Shaw, who dropped the boat to Mikes, passed away in 1991. Radioman Leverle Westerman is retired and resides in Evans City, Pennsylvania. John C. Sellman (plane captain aboard Pflum's PB4Y-2) resides in Vancouver, Washington. Howard Commons, (radioman aboard DANGEROUS DAN), resides in Central Point, Oregon. Bill Satzer spent his career with the U.S. Treasury Department as an IRS agent and now lives in retirement in Minnesota. Raymond J. Pflum, who led the Privateers in the rescue of Ed Mikes, retired as a rear admiral in 1957. He was senior vice president of Allegheny Airlines when he passed away in 1965. Ralph Ettinger, Pflum's wingman, died in 1989. Commander James H. Ashley, Jr. retired as a rear admiral and died on August 4, 1979. The **USS Aspro** (SS-309) was decommissioned and torpedoed for target practice on November 16, 1962.

Radioman Laverle H. Westerman in Bulgin' Bessie heard the call: "Splash in the bay" and the rescue began. (Laverle Westerman)

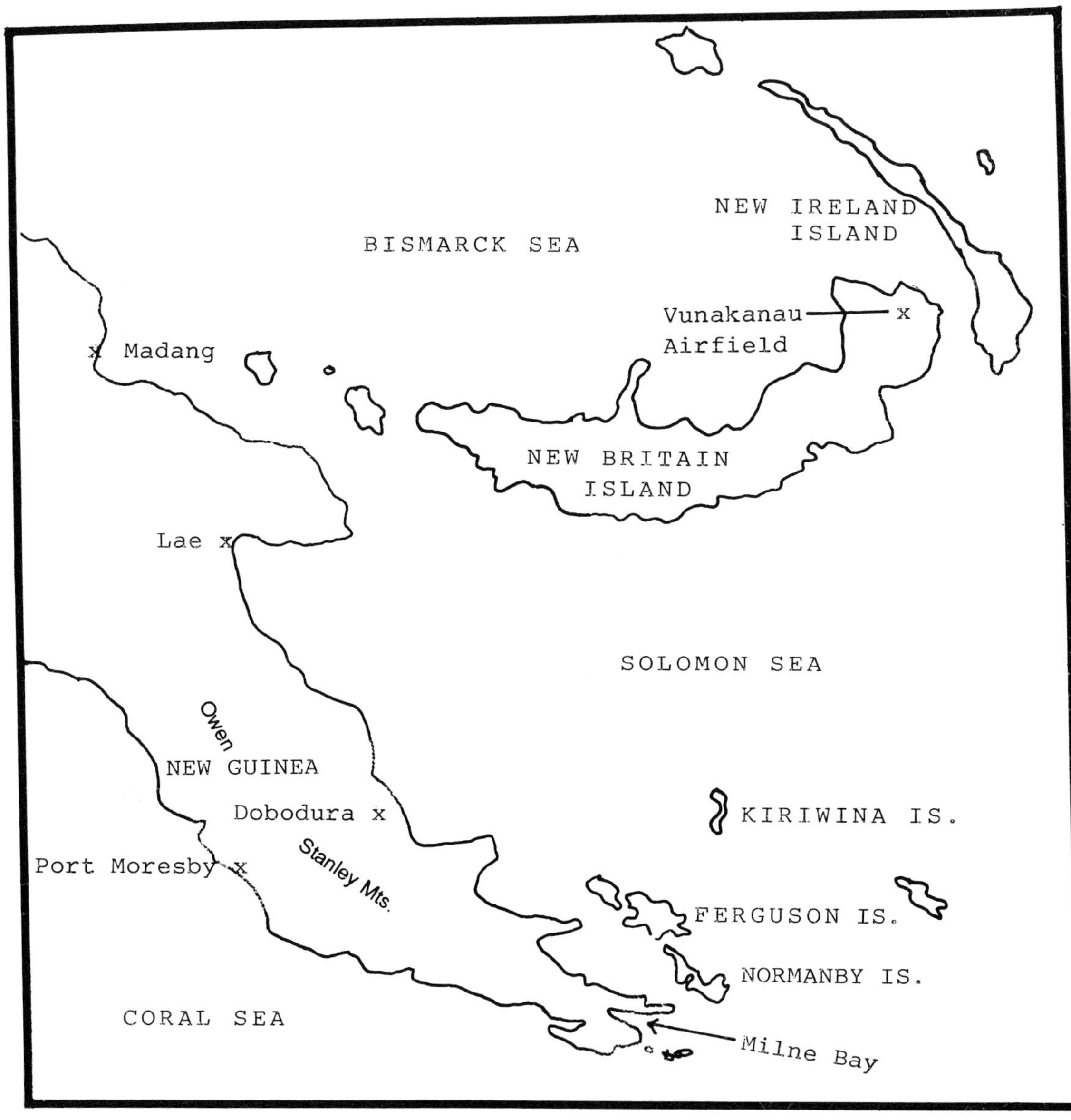

NEW IRELAND ISLAND
BISMARCK SEA
Vunakanau Airfield
Madang
NEW BRITAIN ISLAND
Lae
SOLOMON SEA
Owen
NEW GUINEA
Dobodura
KIRIWINA IS.
Port Moresby
Stanley Mts.
FERGUSON IS.
NORMANBY IS.
CORAL SEA
Milne Bay

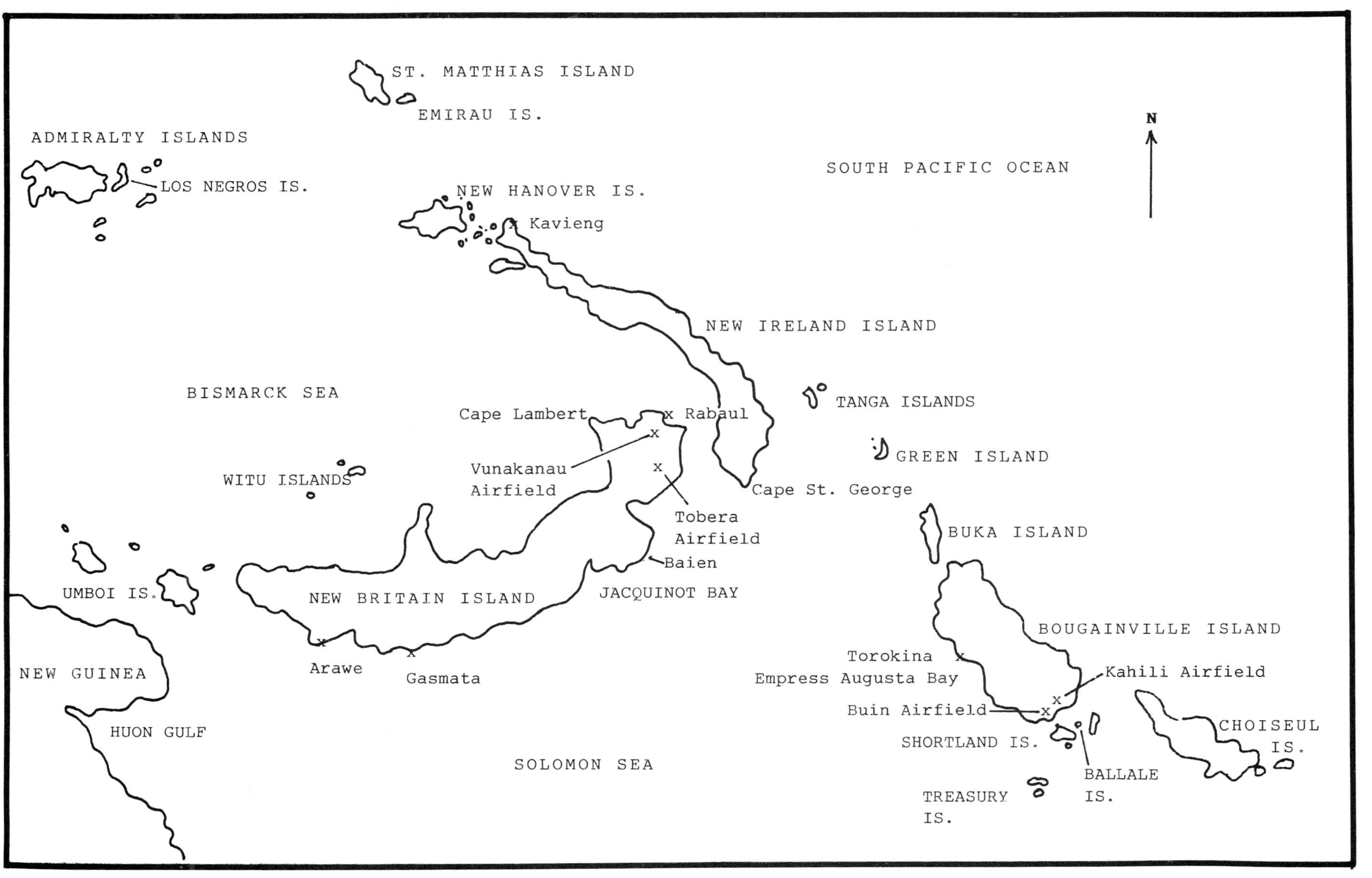
ST. MATTHIAS ISLAND
EMIRAU IS.
ADMIRALTY ISLANDS
LOS NEGROS IS.
NEW HANOVER IS.
Kavieng
SOUTH PACIFIC OCEAN
N
NEW IRELAND ISLAND
BISMARCK SEA
TANGA ISLANDS
Cape Lambert
Rabaul
Vunakanau
Airfield
GREEN ISLAND
WITU ISLANDS
Cape St. George
Tobera
Airfield
BUKA ISLAND
Baien
UMBOI IS.
NEW BRITAIN ISLAND
JACQUINOT BAY
BOUGAINVILLE ISLAND
Torokina
Empress Augusta Bay
Kahili Airfield
NEW GUINEA
Arawe
Gasmata
Buin Airfield
CHOISEUL
IS.
HUON GULF
SHORTLAND IS.
SOLOMON SEA
BALLALE
IS.
TREASURY
IS.

N
Tsuchiura
Kasumigaura
Lake
Konoike Airfield
Kashima Nada
Scamara
Scanlan
Sawara
Machi
Narita
Airfield
Choshi Point
TOKYO
Chiba
Tokyo Bay
Yokohama
Jack Scanlan
parachuted down
and was captured
here.
Sagami Bay

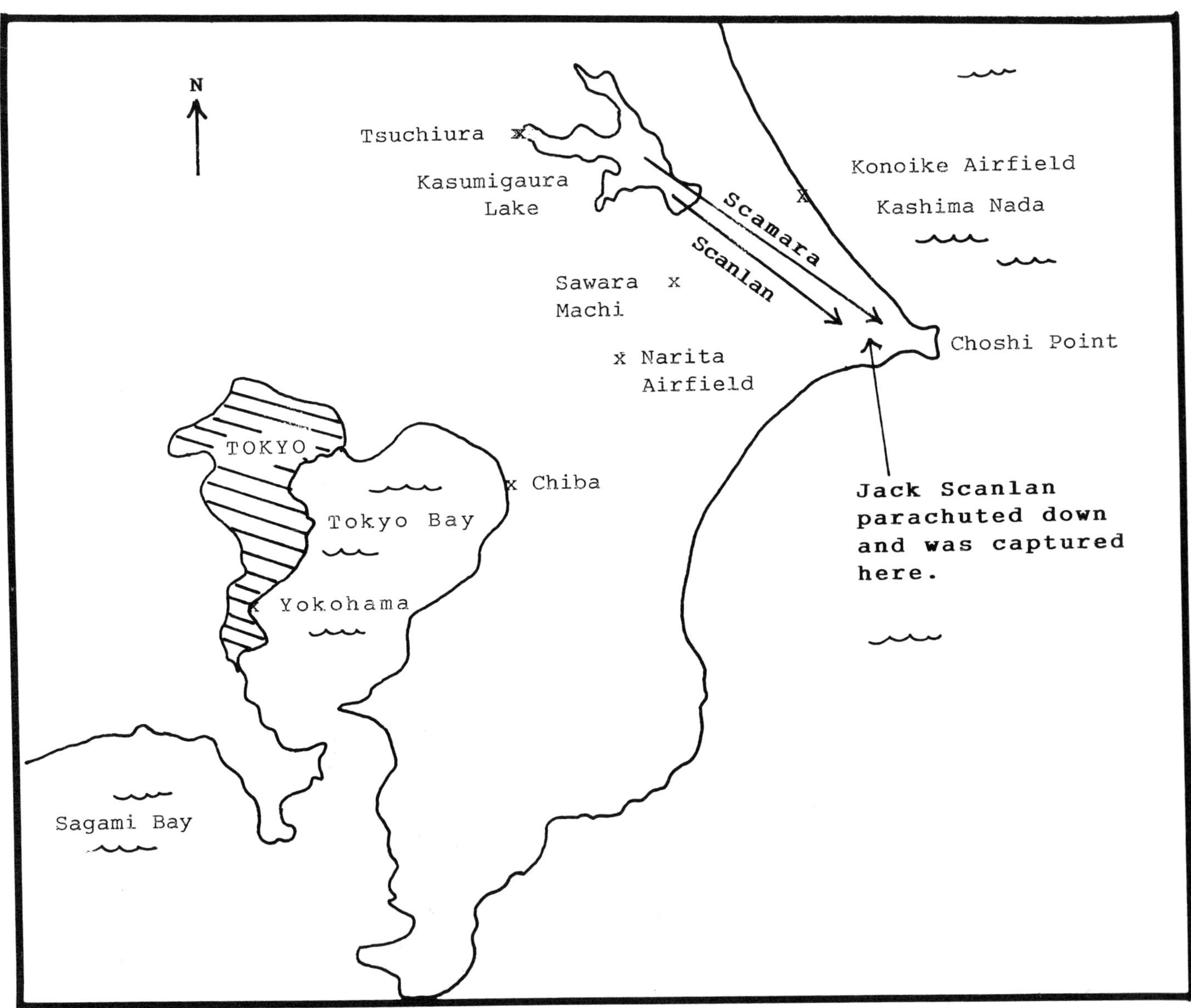

2

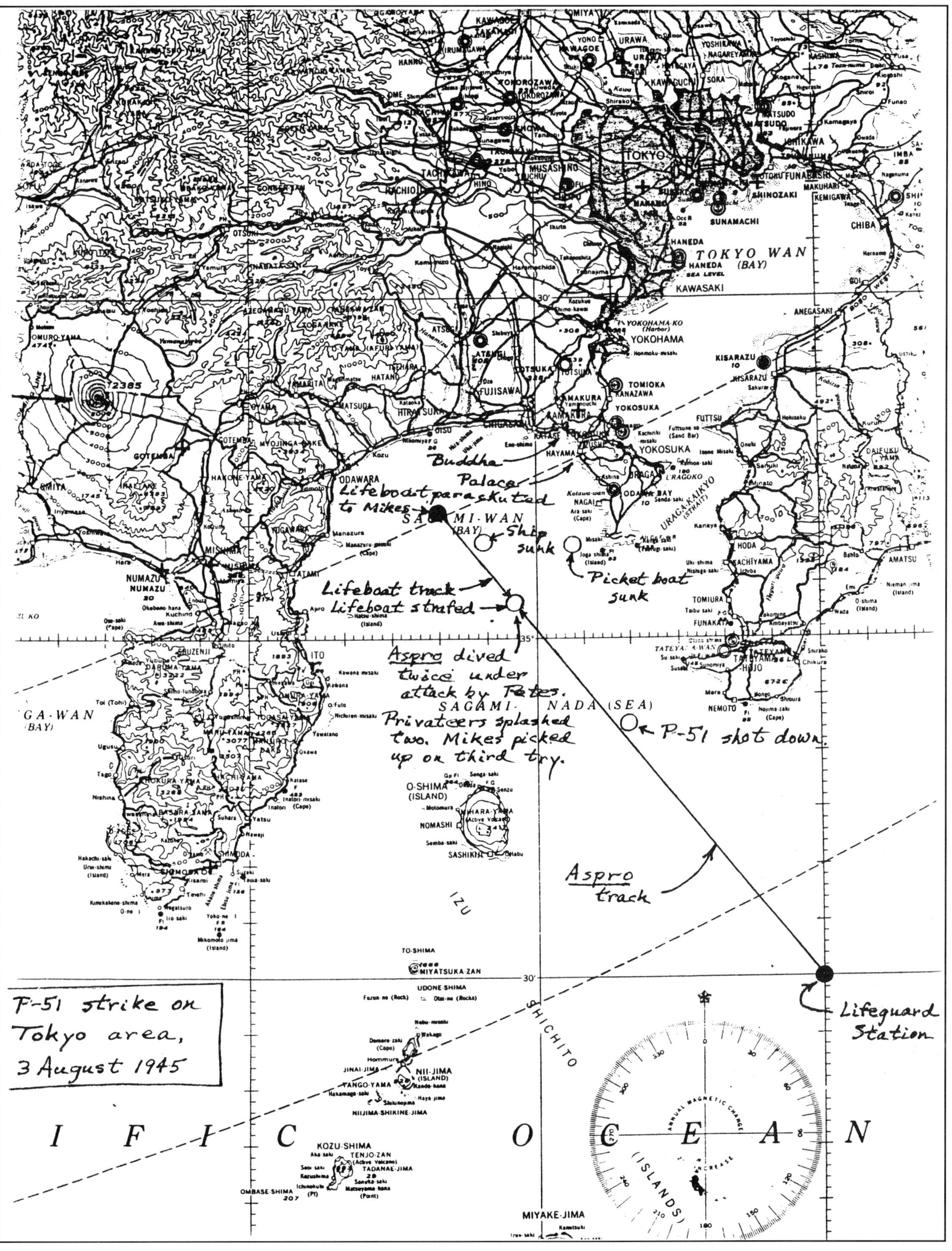
Buddha
Palace
Lifeboat parachuted to Mikes
Ship sunk
Picket boat sunk
Lifeboat track
Lifeboat strafed
Aspro dived twice under attack by Petes. Privateers splashed two. Mikes picked up on third try.
P-51 shot down.
Aspro track
Lifeguard Station
F-51 strike on Tokyo area, 3 August 1945
TOKYO
TOKYO WAN (BAY)
YOKOHAMA
YOKOSUKA
SAGAMI-WAN (BAY)
SAGAMI-NADA (SEA)
O-SHIMA (ISLAND)
IZU
SHICHITO (ISLANDS)
NII-JIMA (ISLAND)
KOZU-SHIMA
MIYAKE-JIMA
I F I C O C E A N

DEFINITIVE MILITARY/AVIATION HISTORIES
By
PHALANX PUBLISHING CO., LTD.

The Pineapple Air Force: Pearl Harbor to Tokyo
by John Lambert $44.95

Republic P-47 Thunderbolt, The Final Chapter: Latin American Air Forces Service
by Dan Hagedorn $14.95

Eagles of Duxford: The 78th Fighter Group in World War II
by Garry Fry $29.95

Kearby's Thunderbolts: The 348th Fighter Group in World War II
by John Stanaway $24.95

Wildcats Over Casablanca
by John Lambert $11.95

B-25 Mitchell, The Magnificent Medium
by Norman L. Avery $29.95

SORTIE:
A bibliography of U.S. Air Force, Navy and Marine combat aviation unit histories from World War II. $10.95

FORTHCOMING TITLES

MESSERSCHMITT ROULETTE;
The Desert War from a Hurricane Recce Pilot of No 451 Squadron RAAF by Wing Commander Geoffrey Morley-Mower, DFC, RAF (ret.)

THE 1ST FIGHTER GROUP IN WORLD WAR II:
The MTO war of the this legendary P-38 unit by one of its pilots, John D. Mullins

THE SUNDOWNERS
World War II history of VF-11 on two combat tours, by Barrett Tillman

FANTAIL FIGHTERS
Battleship and cruiser floatplanes in World War II, by Jerry Scutts

THE YOXFORD BOYS
The 357th Fighter Group in Europe by Merle Olmsted

MARINE MITCHELLS
U.S. Marine Corps operations with PBJ aircraft in the Pacific, by Jerry Scutts.